A STUDY OF REVELATION CHAPTER 14

Salvation, Judgment, and the Victory of Christ in Revelation 14

Dr. Maxwell Shimba

Printed by Shimba Publishing LLC
Printed in the United States of America

TABLE OF CONTENTS

INTRODUCTION

Revelation Chapter 14 - A Vision of Triumph, Judgment, and Endurance

The Book of Revelation, the final book of the New Testament, is often referred to as "The Apocalypse," a term that signifies unveiling or revelation. It is one of the most profound and symbolically rich books in the entire Bible, filled with vivid imagery, prophetic visions, and symbolic language that have fascinated and intrigued scholars, theologians, and believers for centuries. Revelation was written by the Apostle John while exiled on the island of Patmos, likely during a period of intense persecution under Roman rule. It offers a glimpse into the future, revealing the ultimate victory of Christ and the final judgment of the world. While much of Revelation is shrouded in mystery, its central message is clear: God will triumph, evil will be vanquished, and His faithful followers will be rewarded.

Among the 22 chapters in Revelation, Chapter 14 holds a special place. It is a chapter that stands at a critical juncture in John's apocalyptic vision, transitioning from the rise of the beast and the great tribulations in the preceding chapters to the final outpouring of God's wrath and the ultimate victory of Christ in the chapters that follow. Revelation 14 encapsulates the essence of the entire book by emphasizing three core themes: the triumph of the Lamb and His faithful followers, the declaration of impending judgment upon the earth, and the final harvest of the righteous and the wicked.

This chapter opens with a glorious vision of the Lamb standing on Mount Zion, surrounded by 144,000 faithful followers, a group described as those who have been redeemed from the earth. The imagery here is deeply symbolic, with the Lamb representing Jesus Christ and Mount Zion symbolizing God's ultimate reign and authority. This scene offers a glimpse of victory and hope, assuring believers that those who remain steadfast in their faith will share in Christ's triumph. The 144,000, often interpreted as a symbolic number representing the entirety of God's people, are marked by their purity and faithfulness, standing in contrast to the corruption of the world.

However, Revelation 14 is not merely a chapter of hope. It also carries a solemn message of judgment, delivered through the proclamations of three angels. These angelic messengers bring warnings to the inhabitants of the earth, urging them to turn away from evil and worship God. The fall of "Babylon" is foretold, representing the collapse of worldly powers and systems that oppose God. The angels warn against worshiping the beast and receiving its mark, signaling that those who align themselves with evil will face the full wrath of God. This section of the chapter serves as a powerful reminder that God's judgment is imminent and that the choices people make in this life have eternal consequences.

The chapter concludes with two striking images of harvest, a common biblical metaphor for judgment. The first harvest, led by "One like the Son of Man" seated on a cloud, represents the gathering of the righteous into God's kingdom. The second harvest, a grim and bloody scene of grapes being thrown into the winepress of God's wrath, symbolizes the judgment and destruction of the wicked. These dual images of harvest highlight the final separation of the righteous and the wicked, underscoring the urgency of repentance and the importance of remaining faithful to God.

The structure of Revelation Chapter 14 reflects the broader themes found throughout the book of Revelation: hope for the faithful, judgment for the wicked, and a call to endurance. For early Christians facing persecution and hardship, this chapter would have been a source of encouragement and a reminder of God's ultimate plan. It assures believers that despite the trials and tribulations they may endure, Christ's victory is certain, and their faithfulness will be rewarded. At the same time, it serves as a sobering warning to those who choose to follow the ways of the world rather than the ways of God.

In this book, we will explore the profound themes of Revelation Chapter 14 in greater detail. We will examine the significance of the 144,000 and their role as the redeemed of the earth. We will unpack the messages of the three angels and their warnings of impending judgment. Finally, we will delve into the imagery of the final harvest, reflecting on its meaning for the righteous and the wicked. Throughout this journey, we will seek to understand how the messages of Revelation Chapter 14 apply not only to the early Christian church but also to believers today.

This chapter of Revelation offers a powerful combination of hope and warning, of triumph and judgment. It invites us to reflect on the reality of God's coming kingdom and to live with a sense of urgency and faithfulness. As we journey through Revelation 14, may we be reminded of the need to persevere in our faith, to heed God's call to repentance, and to look forward with hope to the day when Christ will return in glory and establish His reign over all the earth.

DR. MAXWELL SHIMBA

CHAPTER 01

THE VISION OF THE 144,000

Revelation 14:1-5 opens with a magnificent and triumphant vision that portrays the Lamb standing on Mount Zion, surrounded by 144,000 faithful followers. This scene offers a stark contrast to the dark and foreboding images of the previous chapters, where the beast and its followers dominate the narrative. Here, John shifts the focus to the victory of Christ and the redemption of His people, offering a glimpse of hope and glory to believers who have endured tribulation.

The Lamb on Mount Zion

The Lamb, as depicted in the Book of Revelation, represents Jesus Christ, often referred to as the "Lamb of God" (John 1:29). In this vision, He stands on Mount Zion, a significant biblical location that holds deep symbolic meaning. In the Old Testament, Mount Zion is often associated with Jerusalem, the city of God, where His presence dwelt in the temple. In the prophetic books, Zion is frequently depicted as the place from which God will reign and bring salvation to His people (Isaiah 2:3, Psalm 2:6). Here in Revelation, Mount Zion takes on a heavenly dimension, symbolizing the ultimate victory and reign of Christ over all creation.

The vision of the Lamb standing on Mount Zion is a powerful image of divine authority and kingship. Unlike the fleeting and corrupt powers of the earth represented by Babylon and the beast, the Lamb's reign is eternal and unshakable. This scene assures the reader that, despite the suffering and persecution faced by the followers of Christ, their ultimate destination is one of victory, where they will stand with the Lamb in His kingdom.

The 144,000: The Redeemed of the Earth

The Lamb is not alone on Mount Zion. He is surrounded by 144,000 individuals, a group described as having "His Father's name written on their foreheads." The symbolic number of 144,000 first appears in Revelation 7, where they are sealed as servants of God from every tribe of Israel. The sealing of the 144,000 indicates God's protection over them, marking them as His own amidst the tribulation that befalls the earth. In Chapter 14, this group reappears, now standing with the Lamb in victory, having remained faithful to God throughout their trials.

The number 144,000 is often understood as symbolic rather than literal. It represents the fullness or completeness of God's people. Some interpret this group as comprising only Jewish believers, while others see it as a symbolic representation of the entire church—both Jews and Gentiles—who have been redeemed by Christ. Regardless of the specific interpretation, what is clear is that this group is marked by their loyalty and devotion to God.

The description of the 144,000 highlights their purity and holiness. They are described as those "who have not defiled themselves with women, for they are virgins" (Revelation 14:4). This imagery of sexual purity is likely symbolic, referring not to physical virginity but to spiritual faithfulness. In the Old Testament, idolatry and unfaithfulness to God are often described in terms of sexual immorality (Ezekiel 16, Hosea 1-3). Thus, the 144,000 are those who have remained faithful to God, rejecting the false gods and immoral practices of the world.

These individuals are further described as those who "follow the Lamb wherever He goes." Their faithfulness is marked not only by their resistance to worldly temptations but by their active obedience and commitment to Christ. They are wholly devoted to Him, willing to follow Him even into suffering and tribulation. This characteristic of the 144,000 serves as a model for all believers, emphasizing the call to discipleship and the importance of following Christ with unwavering faith.

The 144,000 are also described as the "firstfruits to God and to the Lamb" (Revelation 14:4). In biblical tradition, the firstfruits were the first portion of the harvest offered to God, symbolizing dedication and thanksgiving. By calling the 144,000 the firstfruits, John underscores that they are the first of the redeemed, the initial gathering of God's people who will inherit the blessings of His kingdom. Their faithfulness in the face of adversity sets them apart as an offering to God, and they serve as a sign of the greater harvest of souls yet to come.

Finally, the 144,000 are marked by their speech: "And in their mouth was found no deceit, for they are without fault before the throne of God" (Revelation 14:5). This description emphasizes their moral integrity. Their words and actions align with their faith, and they are free from falsehood or hypocrisy. Their blamelessness before God reflects the transformative power of Christ's redemption, which enables them to stand pure and righteous before His throne.

The New Song of the Redeemed

In this vision, the 144,000 are heard singing a "new song before the throne" (Revelation 14:3). The concept of a new song is significant in biblical literature, often symbolizing a fresh outpouring of praise in response to God's redemptive work (Psalm 96:1, Isaiah 42:10). The new song sung by the 144,000 is one that no one else can learn, underscoring the unique experience and testimony of those who have been redeemed from the earth.

The fact that only the 144,000 can sing this song indicates that their experience of redemption is distinct. They have endured the great tribulation, resisted the temptations of the world, and remained faithful to Christ. Their song is a personal expression of their journey with the Lamb, and it stands as a testimony to God's grace and power in their lives.

The sound of the song is described as being "like the voice of many waters, and like the voice of loud thunder" (Revelation 14:2). This vivid imagery conveys the magnitude and majesty of the song, a powerful chorus of praise that resonates throughout heaven. It is accompanied by the sound of harps, instruments often associated with worship and celebration in Scripture (Psalm 33:2, Revelation 5:8).

Spiritual Implications of the Vision

The vision of the 144,000 standing with the Lamb on Mount Zion holds deep spiritual significance for believers. First and foremost, it reminds Christians that faithfulness to God will be rewarded. Despite the trials and tribulations that believers may face in this world, their ultimate destiny is to stand with Christ in victory. This scene offers a foretaste of the future kingdom, where God's people will reign with Him in glory.

Moreover, the 144,000 serve as a model of what it means to be a follower of Christ. Their purity, faithfulness, and commitment to the Lamb are qualities that all believers are called to emulate. In a world filled with distractions, temptations, and pressures to conform, the 144,000 demonstrate the importance of remaining true to God, even when it comes at great personal cost.

Finally, the vision of the new song reminds believers of the power of worship and the importance of giving thanks to God for His redemptive work. The 144,000 sing a song that no one else can learn, a testimony of their unique experience of God's grace. Similarly, every believer has a personal testimony of God's work in their life, and worship becomes an opportunity to express gratitude and praise for His faithfulness.

Revelation 14:1-5 provides a striking image of the Lamb and His faithful followers standing in victory on Mount Zion. The 144,000, marked by their purity, faithfulness, and devotion to Christ, represent the redeemed of the earth who have persevered through tribulation. Their new song of praise reflects their unique testimony of God's grace and power. As believers today, this vision offers both encouragement and a call to live with steadfast faith, knowing that the reward for those who follow the Lamb is to stand with Him in His kingdom.

Mount Zion and the Lamb

In Revelation 14:1, the Apostle John describes a profound vision of Mount Zion and the Lamb, an image that is rich with biblical symbolism and meaning. This scene serves as a pivotal moment in the Book of Revelation, offering hope and assurance to believers by emphasizing the ultimate victory of Christ over the forces of evil. To fully grasp the depth of this vision, we must first understand the significance of Mount Zion and the Lamb in the broader context of Scripture.

Mount Zion: The Heavenly Jerusalem

Mount Zion holds a special place in both the Old and New Testaments, symbolizing God's dwelling place and His kingdom. In the Old Testament, Mount Zion initially referred to the physical hill in Jerusalem where David established his stronghold (2 Samuel 5:7), but over time, Zion came to represent more than just a geographic location. It became a symbol of God's presence with His people and His ultimate rule over all the earth.

As the seat of God's temple in Jerusalem, Zion was associated with divine authority, worship, and blessing. The prophets frequently spoke of Zion as the place from which God would rule and bring justice and salvation to His people. Isaiah, for instance, writes, "For out of Zion shall go forth the law, and the word of the Lord from Jerusalem" (Isaiah 2:3). Similarly, the Psalms describe Zion as the city of God, "beautiful in elevation, the joy of all the earth" (Psalm 48:2).

In the New Testament, however, the concept of Mount Zion takes on a more heavenly meaning. The author of Hebrews 12:22 describes Mount Zion as the "heavenly Jerusalem," the place where the redeemed gather in the presence of God. This spiritual Zion is contrasted with the earthly city of Jerusalem, pointing to the eternal city where God's ultimate reign will be fully realized. Thus, in the vision of Revelation 14, Mount Zion represents not just a physical location, but the heavenly city of God, where Christ reigns in His full glory and authority.

John's vision of the Lamb standing on Mount Zion emphasizes the fulfillment of these prophecies. It is a declaration that Christ, the Lamb who was slain for the sins of the world, is now victorious. He stands on Zion as the ruler and redeemer, having conquered sin, death, and the forces of evil. Zion, in this context, symbolizes the final and eternal reign of God's kingdom, where the faithful will dwell with Him forever.

The Lamb: Jesus Christ, the Victorious Savior

The image of the Lamb in the Book of Revelation is one of the most profound and central symbols of Christ. Throughout Revelation, the Lamb represents Jesus Christ, particularly focusing on His sacrificial role in the redemption of humanity. As the Lamb of God, Jesus offered Himself as the ultimate sacrifice to atone for the sins of the world, a fulfillment of the Old Testament sacrificial system.

The Lamb imagery has deep roots in the Old Testament. The Passover lamb in Exodus (Exodus 12:1-13) was slain to protect the Israelites from God's judgment, and the blood of the lamb was a sign that spared the people from destruction. Similarly, the prophet Isaiah foretold of a suffering servant who would be led "like a lamb to the slaughter" (Isaiah 53:7), taking upon Himself the sins of many. In the New Testament, John the Baptist explicitly identifies Jesus as the Lamb of God who "takes away the sin of the world" (John 1:29).

In Revelation, the Lamb is often depicted as both slain and triumphant. In Revelation 5:6, John sees the Lamb standing "as though it had been slain," emphasizing that Christ's victory came through His death on the cross.

However, the Lamb is not powerless; rather, His sacrificial death is the source of His authority and victory. As the one who was slain, He is now exalted, receiving worship and praise from all creation (Revelation 5:12-13).

In Revelation 14, the Lamb stands on Mount Zion, not as a suffering servant but as a victorious king. This image powerfully combines both aspects of Christ's identity: the Lamb who was sacrificed and the King who now reigns. His position on Mount Zion indicates that His victory is complete, and He now rules over His people with divine authority.

Christ's Victory and Divine Authority

The vision of the Lamb standing on Mount Zion serves as a declaration of Christ's ultimate victory. While the previous chapters of Revelation described the rise of the beast and the persecution of God's people, this vision shifts the focus to the triumph of the Lamb and His faithful followers. The Lamb's victory is not just over earthly powers but over sin, death, and all the spiritual forces of evil that stand in opposition to God's kingdom.

This victorious image of Christ standing on Mount Zion is also a picture of divine rulership. The Lamb is not just a symbol of sacrifice but of kingship. In biblical thought, Mount Zion represents the throne of God's rule, and by standing on Zion, the Lamb is depicted as the ruler of God's eternal kingdom. He is the King of kings and Lord of lords (Revelation 19:16), the one who has been given all authority in heaven and on earth (Matthew 28:18).

Moreover, the Lamb is not alone on Mount Zion. He is surrounded by 144,000 followers, a group that represents those who have remained faithful to Him through tribulation. These followers bear the name of God and the Lamb on their foreheads, symbolizing their allegiance and belonging to Christ. Their presence with the Lamb on Zion underscores the promise of victory for the faithful. Despite the trials and tribulations they have faced, they now share in Christ's victory and stand with Him in His kingdom.

The vision of the Lamb on Mount Zion also serves as a fulfillment of biblical prophecy. The prophets often spoke of a future time when God's anointed king would reign from Zion and bring peace and justice to the earth. In Psalm 2:6, God declares, "I have installed my King on Zion, my holy mountain." This messianic prophecy finds its ultimate fulfillment in Christ, who, as the Lamb, now stands in triumph on Zion, ruling with justice and righteousness.

Theological and Spiritual Significance

The imagery of the Lamb standing on Mount Zion carries profound theological and spiritual significance for believers. First and foremost, it is a message of hope and assurance. For Christians enduring persecution or suffering, this vision offers a powerful reminder that Christ has already won the victory. No matter how bleak the present circumstances may appear, the final outcome is secure: Christ will reign, and His people will share in His victory.

Additionally, the vision of the Lamb on Zion serves as a call to faithfulness and perseverance. The 144,000 who stand with the Lamb are those who have remained faithful to Him, even in the face of great tribulation. They have resisted the pressures of the world and the temptations to follow the beast, and now they stand victorious with Christ. This encourages believers to remain steadfast in their faith, knowing that their perseverance will be rewarded in the end.

Finally, the vision highlights the central role of Christ's sacrificial death in God's plan of redemption. The Lamb stands as both the suffering servant and the reigning king, demonstrating that the path to victory lies through the cross. Christ's death and resurrection are the means by which He has triumphed over sin and death, and His followers are called to follow in His footsteps, embracing both suffering and the hope of resurrection.

The vision of Mount Zion and the Lamb in Revelation 14:1 is a profound declaration of Christ's victory and the promise of redemption for His people. Mount Zion symbolizes the heavenly Jerusalem, the city of God, where

Christ reigns with divine authority. The Lamb, representing Jesus Christ, stands as both the sacrificial Savior and the triumphant King. This vision offers believers hope, assurance, and a call to faithfulness, reminding them that no matter the trials they face, Christ's victory is certain, and they are called to share in His reign.

The 144,000

In Revelation 14:1-5, the Apostle John provides a vision of the Lamb standing on Mount Zion with 144,000 followers. This group, marked by their purity and devotion, represents the redeemed who stand with Christ in triumph. The number 144,000 is highly symbolic and has been the subject of extensive theological interpretation. In this section, we will explore the various meanings behind this number, the identity of the 144,000, and the spiritual significance of their characteristics.

The Symbolism of the 144,000

The number 144,000 appears earlier in Revelation, specifically in Revelation 7:4, where 12,000 individuals from each of the twelve tribes of Israel are sealed by God during a time of great tribulation. The number 144,000 is generally understood as symbolic rather than literal, representing the fullness or completeness of God's people. This number is a product of 12 multiplied by 12,000, with the number 12 symbolizing divine perfection, organization, and God's covenant with His people. It reflects a sense of completeness, emphasizing the idea that all of God's people—both Jews and Gentiles—are included in His plan of redemption.

Some theologians interpret the 144,000 as representing the totality of God's people throughout history, encompassing both Israel and the Church. In this view, the 144,000 includes the faithful followers of Christ from all nations and peoples, not limited to a specific ethnic or religious group. This interpretation aligns with the broader themes of Revelation, where the Gospel message is extended to all tribes, tongues, and nations (Revelation 7:9).

Others see the 144,000 as a reference specifically to Jewish believers who have remained faithful to Christ during the great tribulation. In this interpretation, the number signifies a remnant of Israel who have been sealed and protected by God during the end times. This view is rooted in Old Testament prophecies, such as those found in Isaiah and Zechariah, which speak of a faithful remnant of Israel who will be preserved and restored in the last days.

Regardless of the specific interpretation, the key message is that the 144,000 represent those who have remained faithful to God and have been sealed with His protection. Their presence with the Lamb on Mount Zion is a testament to their perseverance and faithfulness, even in the face of great trials and persecution.

The Sealing of the 144,000

One of the defining characteristics of the 144,000 is that they have been sealed with the name of God on their foreheads (Revelation 14:1). This seal signifies God's protection and ownership, marking them as His people in contrast to those who bear the mark of the beast. In ancient times, a seal was used to denote authority, ownership, and protection, and in this context, it represents God's commitment to preserve and protect His faithful followers.

The sealing of the 144,000 serves as a counterpart to the mark of the beast found in Revelation 13:16-17. While the mark of the beast symbolizes allegiance to the forces of evil and rebellion against God, the seal of God represents allegiance to Christ and divine protection from the coming judgment. Those who are sealed by God are spared from His wrath and are promised eternal life in His kingdom.

This concept of sealing also draws from Old Testament imagery. For instance, in Ezekiel 9:4-6, God commands an angel to place a mark on the foreheads of the righteous in Jerusalem, sparing them from the destruction that would befall the wicked. Similarly, in Revelation, the 144,000 are sealed as a sign of their righteousness and their protection from the judgment that is about to be unleashed upon the earth.

The Purity of the 144,000

In Revelation 14:4, the 144,000 are described as those "who have not defiled themselves with women, for they are virgins." This statement has led to various interpretations, many of which emphasize the spiritual purity of the 144,000 rather than focusing on their physical condition.

The phrase "not defiled themselves with women" should not be taken as a condemnation of marriage or sexual relations within marriage. Rather, it is likely symbolic of their spiritual purity and faithfulness to God. In biblical imagery, sexual immorality is often used metaphorically to describe idolatry and spiritual unfaithfulness. For example, the Old Testament frequently uses the metaphor of adultery to describe Israel's unfaithfulness to God when they worshiped idols or engaged in pagan practices (Jeremiah 3:6-9, Ezekiel 16).

Thus, the description of the 144,000 as virgins points to their spiritual integrity and their refusal to engage in idolatry or compromise with the corrupt systems of the world. They are a people who have remained faithful to God, resisting the temptations and allurements of the world, including the worship of the beast and participation in its immoral practices. Their spiritual purity sets them apart as a holy and devoted people, fully consecrated to God.

This purity is further emphasized by their relationship with the Lamb. The 144,000 are described as those who "follow the Lamb wherever He goes" (Revelation 14:4). This statement highlights their complete devotion to Christ, their willingness to obey Him, and their steadfast commitment to follow Him even through suffering and tribulation. Their faithfulness is not passive but active, as they continually follow the Lamb, walking in His footsteps of righteousness and obedience.

The Firstfruits of the Harvest

In Revelation 14:4, the 144,000 are also described as the firstfruits to God and to the Lamb. This term, firstfruits, carries significant biblical meaning. In the Old Testament, the firstfruits were the first portion of the harvest that was offered to God as a sign of dedication and gratitude (Leviticus 23:10-14). The firstfruits were seen as holy and set apart, symbolizing the entirety of the harvest that was yet to come.

By describing the 144,000 as firstfruits, John emphasizes that they are a holy offering to God, set apart from the rest of the world. They represent the initial gathering of God's people, the first of many who will be redeemed through Christ's sacrifice. This imagery also points to the greater harvest that is to come, suggesting that the 144,000 are only the beginning of the multitude of souls who will be gathered into God's kingdom.

The use of firstfruits also underscores the special role of the 144,000 in God's plan. Just as the firstfruits were considered sacred, the 144,000 are portrayed as a unique and holy group who have been especially faithful to God. Their dedication and faithfulness serve as a model for all believers, reminding Christians of the importance of living a life that is consecrated to God.

Without Deceit and Blameless Before God

Another characteristic of the 144,000 is that "no lie was found in their mouths; they are blameless" (Revelation 14:5). This description highlights their moral integrity and their commitment to truth. In a world filled with deception, falsehood, and the lies of the beast, the 144,000 stand out as a people of truth. Their words and actions align with their faith, and they live lives of sincerity and righteousness.

The fact that they are described as "blameless" before God suggests that they have been cleansed and made righteous through the blood of the Lamb. This echoes the broader message of Revelation that those who are washed in the blood of the Lamb are made pure and holy, able to stand before God without guilt or shame (Revelation 7:14).

This blamelessness is not a result of their own works but of Christ's redemptive sacrifice. It is through the Lamb that they have been made righteous, and it is through their relationship with Him that they are able to stand faultless before the throne of God. Their blamelessness also reflects their faithfulness in keeping God's commandments and their refusal to compromise with the falsehoods and corruptions of the world.

The 144,000 in Revelation 14 represent the faithful followers of Christ who have remained spiritually pure and devoted to Him throughout the trials and tribulations of the world. They are marked by their purity, faithfulness, and obedience to the Lamb, and they stand as a holy offering to God, the firstfruits of a greater harvest yet to come. Whether seen as a literal group of Jewish believers or as a symbolic representation of the entire body of Christ, the 144,000 serve as a model of what it means to live a life fully consecrated to God.

Their presence with the Lamb on Mount Zion offers believers the promise of victory and redemption, assuring them that those who remain faithful to God will share in Christ's triumph. The 144,000 remind us of the importance of spiritual purity, truthfulness, and perseverance, calling all believers to live lives that are worthy of the Lamb who was slain and who now reigns in glory.

The New Song

In Revelation 14:3, the 144,000 redeemed individuals standing with the Lamb on Mount Zion are described as singing a "new song". This song is a unique and powerful expression of victory and deliverance, one that only the 144,000 can learn. The idea of a new song holds deep biblical significance, as it often represents a response to God's mighty acts of salvation and a testimony of His faithfulness. In this chapter, the new song sung by the 144,000 serves as a profound symbol of their personal redemption and triumph over the world's trials through their faith in Christ.

The Biblical Tradition of the "New Song"

The concept of singing a new song is found throughout the Bible, particularly in the Psalms and prophetic literature. In these contexts, a new song typically arises when God has performed a new act of salvation or deliverance, prompting His people to offer fresh praise in response to His intervention. For example, in Psalm 40:3, the psalmist proclaims, "He put a new song in my mouth, a hymn of praise to our God," after being delivered from a time of great trouble. Similarly, Psalm 96:1 and Psalm 98:1 exhort believers to "sing to the Lord a new song," celebrating God's reign and His righteous deeds.

In these passages, the new song represents a renewed outpouring of worship, arising from a fresh experience of God's grace and power. It is not simply a repetition of old praises but a unique expression of thanksgiving for God's recent actions in the life of His people. The new song signifies the unfolding of God's ongoing work in history, as He continues to intervene, redeem, and restore His people.

In the same way, the new song in Revelation 14:3 reflects the redeeming work of Christ and the unique experiences of the 144,000. It is a song of victory and deliverance, sung in response to their personal experience of salvation and their triumph over the trials of the world. This song is not one that can be sung by just anyone—it is exclusive to the 144,000, indicating that it arises from their particular journey of faith, struggle, and redemption.

The New Song as a Testimony of the Redeemed

The fact that only the 144,000 can learn the new song suggests that it is closely tied to their personal testimony. Each member of this group has undergone significant tribulation and has emerged victorious by remaining faithful to the Lamb. Their song is a reflection of their individual and collective triumph over the trials and temptations they faced in the world.

Throughout the Book of Revelation, the followers of Christ are portrayed as enduring great hardship, including persecution, deception, and pressure to conform to the worship of the beast. The 144,000, however, are those who have persevered through these challenges, maintaining their spiritual purity and their allegiance to Christ. Their new song is a celebration of their deliverance, a unique testimony that reflects the specific victories they have experienced in their journey of faith.

The exclusivity of this song—"no one could learn the song except the 144,000"—underscores the intimate and personal nature of their redemption. Each person's experience of faith, suffering, and deliverance is distinct, and the new song represents this personalized story of victory. In the same way, each believer has a unique testimony of how God has worked in their life, and this testimony forms the foundation of their praise. The 144,000, having walked the difficult path of discipleship, now stand in victory, and their song is the culmination of their faith and perseverance.

A Song of Victory and Deliverance

The new song of the 144,000 is also a song of victory. In the context of Revelation, victory is not defined by worldly success or power but by spiritual faithfulness. The 144,000 have overcome not by force but by remaining loyal to Christ, even in the face of persecution and temptation. Their victory is rooted in their identification with the Lamb, who Himself achieved victory through His sacrificial death and resurrection.

The content of the new song is not detailed in the text, but its meaning is clear: it is a song of deliverance and a declaration of the triumph of God's kingdom. Just as the Israelites sang a song of deliverance after being rescued from Pharaoh's army at the Red Sea (Exodus 15:1-18), so too do the 144,000 sing a new song to celebrate their deliverance from the powers of evil. It is a song that reflects the fulfillment of God's promises, the defeat of the enemies of God's people, and the ultimate redemption that comes through the Lamb.

This song of victory is a foretaste of the final victory that will be fully realized at the end of Revelation when Christ returns to judge the world and establish His eternal kingdom. In this way, the new song anticipates the consummation of all things—the moment when evil will be fully vanquished, and God's people will live in perfect communion with Him.

The Role of Worship in the New Song

The new song also emphasizes the central role of worship in the life of the redeemed. Throughout the Book of

Revelation, worship is a key theme, as the visions repeatedly show the inhabitants of heaven offering praise and adoration to God and the Lamb. The new song sung by the 144,000 is an expression of this worship, as they acknowledge the grace and power of the Lamb who has redeemed them.

Worship in Revelation is not just an act of praise but a declaration of allegiance. To worship God is to declare loyalty to His kingdom and to reject the false systems of power and idolatry represented by the beast and Babylon. The 144,000, by singing their new song, are affirming their commitment to Christ, proclaiming their allegiance to Him as the rightful ruler of the universe.

This act of worship also reflects their gratitude for the Lamb's sacrifice. The fact that the 144,000 have been redeemed "from the earth" indicates that their salvation is the result of Christ's atoning work. Their song is a response to the Lamb's grace, a recognition that their victory and deliverance are entirely the result of His sacrifice and not their own efforts.

In a broader sense, the new song serves as a reminder to all believers of the importance of worshiping God in spirit and truth (John 4:24). As the redeemed sing their song of victory, they point to the ultimate purpose of salvation: to bring glory and honor to God. Worship is not merely an obligation but a joyful response to the incredible gift of salvation that God has provided through Christ.

The New Song as an Eschatological Anthem

Finally, the new song can be seen as an eschatological anthem—a song that points to the end times and the fulfillment of God's redemptive plan. In Revelation, songs often accompany key moments of eschatological significance. For instance, in Revelation 5, the four living creatures and the 24 elders sing a new song when the Lamb is found worthy to open the sealed scroll, signaling the unfolding of God's plan for the end of history.

Similarly, the new song of the 144,000 signifies that a new era is about to begin—the final chapter in the cosmic drama of redemption. Their song marks a transition from the tribulations of the present age to the glorious reign of Christ. It is a song that looks forward to the ultimate fulfillment of God's promises, when His kingdom will be fully established, and His people will experience eternal life in His presence.

In this way, the new song is not only a celebration of past victories but also an expression of hope for the future. It points to the day when all of creation will be restored, and God's people will live in perfect harmony with Him. The 144,000 are the firstfruits of this new creation, and their song anticipates the day when the full harvest of souls will be gathered into God's kingdom.

The new song sung by the 144,000 in Revelation 14:3 is a powerful symbol of victory, deliverance, and worship. It is a unique testimony of the personal triumph of these redeemed individuals, who have remained faithful to Christ through the trials of the world. Their song is a declaration of their allegiance to the Lamb, a celebration of their deliverance from evil, and an expression of worship for the grace and power of God.

As a song of victory, the new song reminds believers that their ultimate hope lies in Christ, whose sacrifice has secured their redemption. It encourages Christians to persevere in faith, knowing that their trials will one day give way to the joy of standing with the Lamb in His kingdom. The new song also calls believers to live lives of worship, continually offering praise and thanksgiving to the God who has redeemed them and is bringing His plan of salvation to its glorious completion.

Spiritual Application

The image of the 144,000 standing with the Lamb on Mount Zion in Revelation 14 provides not only a powerful vision of Christ's ultimate victory but also offers profound spiritual lessons for Christians today. This scene is rich with symbolism that speaks directly to the call for believers to live lives marked by purity, faithfulness, and devotion to Christ. In a world that often pulls people toward temptation, compromise, and worldly pursuits, the example of the 144,000 serves as a reminder of the rewards of perseverance and the ultimate hope of standing with Christ in His eternal kingdom.

A Call to Purity

One of the key characteristics of the 144,000 is their spiritual purity. They are described as those who "have not defiled themselves" and are "blameless" before God (Revelation 14:4-5). In a symbolic sense, this purity reflects their complete devotion to God, free from the corruption and idolatry of the world. For Christians, this is a reminder of the call to live holy and consecrated lives, set apart from the moral compromises that often characterize the world.

The purity of the 144,000 is not merely about external behavior but about the heart's alignment with God's will. It is about rejecting the spiritual compromises that can erode faith—whether that be idolatry, materialism, or moral decay. In a culture where such temptations are ever-present, Christians are called to remain spiritually pure, guarding their hearts and minds from the influences that would lead them away from Christ.

This spiritual purity also speaks to the importance of integrity in the Christian life. The 144,000 are described as those in whom no deceit is found (Revelation 14:5). Their words, actions, and inner lives are consistent with their faith in Christ. Believers are called to strive for the same level of integrity, living in such a way that their faith is not just something they profess but something that is evident in how they live. Living a life of purity means being authentic in faith, refusing to adopt a double life or give in to the pressures of a world that often promotes dishonesty or moral flexibility.

Faithfulness Amid Tribulation

Another key aspect of the 144,000 is their faithfulness. These individuals have persevered through great trials and tribulations, resisting the pressures of the world and remaining loyal to Christ. Revelation 14 describes them as those who "follow the Lamb wherever He goes" (Revelation 14:4). This image of following the Lamb speaks to a life of discipleship, where faithfulness to Christ takes precedence over every other allegiance.

For Christians today, this is a powerful reminder that the Christian walk is not always easy. Believers face various forms of tribulation—whether that be external persecution, societal pressures, or personal struggles. Yet, the vision of the

144,000 encourages believers to remain steadfast in their faith, no matter the cost. Just as the 144,000 refused to bow to the temptations and coercions of the beast, so too are Christians called to endure and resist the forces that would pull them away from Christ.

Faithfulness is not just about surviving hardship; it is about actively following Christ in every aspect of life. The 144,000 are described as following the Lamb "wherever He goes," indicating a deep level of obedience and commitment. This image challenges believers to examine the depth of their own commitment to Christ. Are they willing to follow Him even when it leads through difficult paths? Are they ready to place their trust in Him, even when the journey requires sacrifice or suffering?

Perseverance and Endurance

The 144,000's victory and their position with the Lamb on Mount Zion underscore the importance of perseverance. Revelation repeatedly highlights the need for endurance among the saints (Revelation 13:10; 14:12), especially in the face of overwhelming opposition and tribulation. The 144,000 exemplify this endurance—they did not give up or compromise, even when faced with extreme difficulty.

For modern Christians, this serves as a reminder that faithfulness requires perseverance. The path of discipleship is often long and challenging, and believers must be prepared to face setbacks, trials, and even persecution. Yet, the image of the 144,000 standing with the Lamb offers hope: those who persevere will ultimately share in Christ's victory.

Endurance is not simply about enduring suffering but about maintaining a focus on the eternal promises of God. Believers are encouraged to keep their eyes on the ultimate reward—the opportunity to stand with Christ in His kingdom. In a world filled with distractions and temptations, Christians must continually remind themselves that eternal rewards far outweigh the temporary challenges and sufferings of this life.

Living for the Ultimate Reward

The image of the 144,000 on Mount Zion also reminds believers of the ultimate reward awaiting those who remain faithful to Christ. These redeemed individuals stand with the Lamb, sharing in His victory and experiencing the fullness of God's kingdom. This scene points to the eschatological hope that Christians have—the promise that one day, Christ will return, and His people will reign with Him in glory.

This vision encourages believers to live with an eternal perspective. It is easy to become caught up in the challenges, worries, and distractions of the present world, but the vision of the 144,000 reminds Christians that their true home is with Christ in His kingdom. The reward for faithfulness is not found in this world but in the life to come, where believers will experience the joy of standing with the Lamb.

This eternal reward motivates believers to stay focused on their heavenly calling. It reminds them that the temporary trials they face now are preparing them for an eternal glory that far surpasses anything they could imagine. The apostle Paul echoed this truth in his letters, reminding believers that "our present sufferings are not worth comparing with the glory that will be revealed in us" (Romans 8:18). The 144,000 on Mount Zion exemplify this truth, having persevered through hardship and now experiencing the joy of God's presence.

Following the Lamb

Perhaps the most significant spiritual application of the 144,000 is their complete devotion to the Lamb. They are described as those who "follow the Lamb wherever He goes," a phrase that encapsulates the essence of Christian discipleship. Following Christ means more than just intellectual belief; it requires a deep, personal commitment to live according to His teachings and to remain loyal to Him in every circumstance.

For believers today, this call to follow the Lamb is as relevant as ever. In a world filled with competing loyalties and distractions, Christians are reminded to make Christ the central focus of their lives. Following the Lamb means aligning one's heart, mind, and actions with the will of Christ. It means daily choosing to prioritize Him over the demands of the world.

This following is not just during moments of ease but also through times of trial. The 144,000 remained faithful through the most intense periods of tribulation, and their example challenges believers to follow Christ unwaveringly, no matter the cost. It is through this kind of faithful following that believers will ultimately stand with the Lamb in victory.

The image of the 144,000 on Mount Zion presents Christians with a powerful vision of victory, faithfulness, and hope. It serves as a reminder that in a world filled with temptation, tribulation, and distractions, believers are called to live lives of purity, perseverance, and complete devotion to Christ. The 144,000 offer a model for Christian discipleship—remaining faithful through trials, following the Lamb wherever He leads, and living in anticipation of the ultimate reward of standing with Him in His kingdom.

For today's believers, this vision is both an encouragement and a challenge. It encourages Christians to hold fast to their faith, knowing that their ultimate reward is eternal life with Christ. At the same time, it challenges them to live lives that reflect their allegiance to Christ, demonstrating spiritual purity, perseverance, and unwavering commitment in all aspects of life.

CHAPTER 02

THE THREE ANGELIC MESSAGES

The second section of Revelation 14 (verses 6-13) presents a striking and solemn series of warnings delivered by three angels. These angelic proclamations are significant in the unfolding narrative of the Book of Revelation, as they deliver final calls for repentance and announce the coming judgment of God upon the earth. The three messages stand as urgent reminders to humanity of the spiritual choices that must be made in the face of the impending wrath of God.

This chapter serves as a critical turning point in Revelation's overall structure, where the focus shifts from a vision of the redeemed standing victorious with the Lamb to the fate of those who have not yet repented. The three angels bring warnings that stress the importance of worshiping the one true God, renouncing allegiance to the beast, and preparing for the outpouring of divine judgment. Each angel's message carries its own unique warning, but together, they highlight the spiritual gravity of the moment and the necessity for people to make a decision about where their loyalties lie.

The First Angel: The Proclamation of the Everlasting Gospel

Revelation 14:6-7 introduces the first angel, who flies in mid-heaven, bringing an urgent message of the "everlasting gospel" to all nations, tribes, languages, and peoples. This angelic proclamation is global in scope, emphasizing that the message of salvation is for all of humanity, regardless of race, ethnicity, or background. The angel's message is described as an eternal gospel, underscoring the fact that this good news is timeless and that God's offer of salvation is constant.

The gospel proclaimed by the first angel is both a message of grace and a warning of judgment. The angel calls on all people to "Fear God and give Him glory, for the hour of His judgment has come" (Revelation 14:7). This is a call to worship the Creator, the one true God who made "heaven and earth, the sea and the springs of water." By invoking creation, the angel emphasizes God's sovereignty over all things, reminding humanity that the God who created the world has the authority to judge it.

This message is reminiscent of the prophetic calls to repentance found throughout Scripture. The prophet Jonah, for example, delivered a similar message to Nineveh, warning the people to repent before God's judgment came upon them (Jonah 3:4). Here, in Revelation 14, the first angel calls the inhabitants of the earth to repent and turn back to God before it is too late.

The Urgency of Worship

The first angel's message underscores the importance of worship. In Revelation, worship is a central theme, and the choice between worshiping God or worshiping the beast is the ultimate dividing line between salvation and destruction. The angel urges humanity to "fear God and give Him glory," calling people to recognize God's holiness, sovereignty, and authority. This fear is not merely terror but a deep reverence and awe for God as the Creator and Judge.

The command to worship God is especially urgent because the hour of judgment has come. The language of judgment implies that the time for decision is running out, and the window of opportunity for repentance is closing. The first angel's message is both an invitation and a warning—inviting people to turn to God in worship while also warning them that the time for repentance is limited.

The call to worship the Creator is a stark contrast to the worship of the beast, which is described earlier in

Revelation (Revelation 13:12-15). Those who worship the beast are aligning themselves with the forces of evil and rebellion against God. In contrast, the angel's message offers humanity the chance to align with the one true God, the Creator of all things, and to acknowledge His rightful place as the object of worship.

The Second Angel: The Fall of Babylon

In Revelation 14:8, the second angel follows the first, declaring a solemn and prophetic statement: "Babylon is fallen, is fallen, that great city, because she has made all nations drink of the wine of the wrath of her fornication." This is the first explicit reference to Babylon in Revelation, though Babylon will be developed more fully in later chapters (Revelation 17-18). Here, Babylon represents a corrupt system of worldly power, idolatry, and immorality that stands in opposition to God and His kingdom.

The fall of Babylon is a symbolic declaration of the impending judgment on the world's systems of sin and rebellion. In the Old Testament, Babylon was a literal city and empire that embodied pride, oppression, and idolatry (Isaiah 13-14, Jeremiah 50-51). In the context of Revelation, however, Babylon symbolizes the worldly powers and systems that lead people away from God, promoting materialism, immorality, and spiritual adultery.

The second angel's message is a declaration of Babylon's inevitable destruction. This great city has seduced the nations, leading them into spiritual fornication—a metaphor for idolatry and unfaithfulness to God. The wine of her fornication represents the intoxicating allure of sin and rebellion that Babylon offers to the world. Through her influence, the nations have turned away from God and have embraced the corrupt values of Babylon.

The announcement of Babylon's fall serves as a warning to all who have aligned themselves with the corrupt systems of the world. It is a reminder that no earthly power or empire can stand against the judgment of God. Though Babylon may appear strong and influential, her fall is certain. The angel's message echoes the Old Testament prophecies of Babylon's fall, such as Isaiah's pronouncement that "Babylon, the jewel of kingdoms, the pride and glory of the Babylonians, will be overthrown by God like Sodom and Gomorrah" (Isaiah 13:19).

For Christians, the second angel's message serves as a reminder to avoid spiritual compromise with the world. Babylon represents the seductions of wealth, power, and immorality that can draw believers away from their allegiance to God. The fall of Babylon warns that those who place their trust in the world's systems will ultimately face destruction, while those who remain faithful to God will be vindicated.

The Third Angel: The Warning Against Worshiping the Beast

The third angel's message, found in Revelation 14:9-11, is the most severe and sobering of the three. This angel delivers a dire warning to anyone who worships the beast and receives its mark: "If anyone worships the beast and its image and receives its mark on their forehead or on their hand, they too will drink the wine of God's fury, which has been poured full strength into the cup of his wrath" (Revelation 14:9-10).

This message builds on the earlier warnings about the mark of the beast in Revelation 13. Those who worship the beast and receive its mark are aligning themselves with the forces of evil and rejecting God's rule. The third angel warns that those who make this choice will face the full wrath of God, which is described in vivid terms. The "wine of God's fury" is a symbol of His righteous anger against sin and rebellion. The image of wine being poured "full strength" into the cup of wrath emphasizes the severity and finality of God's judgment.

The fate of those who worship the beast is described in terrifying detail. They will be tormented with burning sulfur in the presence of the holy angels and the Lamb, and the "smoke of their torment will rise forever and ever" (Revelation 14:10-11). This language reflects the eternal consequences of rejecting God and choosing to worship the beast. The torment is described as unending, signifying that the judgment on those who reject God is both severe and eternal.

The third angel's message is a final warning to those who are still undecided about where their allegiance lies. It underscores the eternal consequences of worshiping the beast and receiving its mark. The starkness of this warning reflects the seriousness of the choice that humanity must make. Those who align with the beast will face God's wrath, while those who remain faithful to God will receive salvation.

The Call to Endurance

In Revelation 14:12-13, following the three angelic messages, there is a brief pause where John offers a word of encouragement to the faithful. He writes: "Here is the patience of the saints; here are those who keep the commandments of God and the faith of Jesus." This statement serves as a reminder that the call to remain faithful to God in the midst of tribulation requires endurance and perseverance.

The warnings delivered by the three angels are not only for those who have not repented but also serve as an encouragement to believers to remain steadfast in their faith. The saints are those who keep God's commandments and hold fast to their faith in Christ, even in the face of persecution and the pressures to conform to the world. The call to patience and endurance is a central theme in Revelation, as believers are continually urged to stay faithful, knowing that their perseverance will be rewarded.

In verse 13, John also records a comforting message for those who face martyrdom: "Blessed are the dead who die in the Lord from now on." This blessing assures believers that those who die in faith will be rewarded with eternal rest. Their works will follow them, meaning that their faithful deeds will not be forgotten, and they will be welcomed into God's eternal kingdom.

The three angelic messages in Revelation 14 serve as a powerful and urgent call to repentance, worship, and faithfulness. The first angel announces the everlasting gospel, reminding humanity to worship God and give Him glory before the final judgment arrives. The second angel declares the fall of Babylon, warning that the corrupt systems of the world will not stand in the face of God's judgment. The third angel delivers a severe warning against worshiping the beast, emphasizing the eternal consequences of rejecting God and aligning with evil.

For believers, these messages are a reminder of the importance of worshiping God alone, avoiding compromise with the world, and remaining faithful to Christ no matter the cost. The call to endurance and the promise of eternal rest for those who die in the Lord serve as encouragements to persevere through trials, knowing that their faithfulness will be rewarded in God's eternal kingdom.

The First Angel - The Everlasting Gospel

In Revelation 14:6-7, the Apostle John describes the appearance of the first of three angels, delivering a powerful and urgent message to the world. This angel flies "in midair," symbolizing its visibility and universal scope, and it carries the proclamation of the "everlasting gospel". The message is directed to "every nation, tribe, tongue, and people", emphasizing its global reach. This angel's proclamation serves as both a final call to humanity to turn to God and an urgent warning that the time for repentance is quickly running out.

The Everlasting Gospel: A Message of Hope and Judgment

The message of the first angel is identified as the everlasting gospel. The term "gospel" refers to the good news of salvation that has been central to the Christian faith since the ministry of Jesus. The gospel proclaims that through the life, death, and resurrection of Christ, humanity is offered forgiveness of sins and the promise of eternal life. In this context, the "everlasting" nature of the gospel emphasizes that this message is eternal and unchanging. It has been God's plan for humanity throughout history and remains the key to salvation in the face of impending judgment.

However, in the context of Revelation 14, the gospel is more than just a message of salvation; it also serves as a final warning. As the world approaches the time of God's final judgment, this proclamation becomes a last opportunity for people to repent and turn to God. The call to repentance, often present in the gospel message, takes on heightened urgency in this passage. The angel announces that the "hour of His judgment has come" (Revelation 14:7), signaling that the period of grace is nearing its end. Those who continue to reject God's call will face His imminent and righteous judgment.

This combination of hope and warning reflects the dual nature of the gospel. For those who accept the message and turn to God, the gospel remains the ultimate message of hope and salvation. It offers the promise of eternal life, reconciliation with God, and freedom from the judgment to come. But for those who reject the message, it becomes a harbinger of judgment. The angel's proclamation serves as a reminder that while God's grace is abundant, it is not infinite; the time to respond to the gospel is limited.

Worshiping the Creator

The central theme of the angel's message is a call to worship the Creator. The angel declares, "Fear God and give Him glory, because the hour of His judgment has come. Worship Him who made the heavens, the earth, the sea, and the springs of water" (Revelation 14:7). This call to worship emphasizes God's sovereignty as the Creator of all things. The phrase "heavens, the earth, the sea, and the springs of water" reflects the totality of creation, reminding humanity that God alone is the source of life and the ruler of the universe.

In the context of Revelation, this call to worship stands in direct opposition to the worship of the beast described in earlier chapters. The world is presented with a stark choice: to either worship God, the true Creator, or to align with the beast and the false systems of power and idolatry it represents. The angel's message reminds humanity that their allegiance must be to God alone, not to the corrupt and temporary powers of the world.

The command to "fear God" is a call to recognize God's holiness, authority, and judgment. The concept of fearing God in Scripture often refers not to being terrified of Him, but to having a deep reverence, awe, and respect for His majesty and righteousness. To fear God is to acknowledge His rightful place as the sovereign ruler of the universe and to respond in humble worship and obedience.

The angel's message also calls people to "give Him glory"—to honor God with their lives, words, and actions. In contrast to the self-glorifying tendencies of the beast and the corrupt powers of the world, this call to give glory to God is a reminder that all honor and praise belong to the Creator alone. Giving glory to God means acknowledging His greatness and submitting to His will.

The Imminent Hour of Judgment

The urgency of the first angel's message is underscored by the declaration that "the hour of His judgment has come" (Revelation 14:7). This phrase signals that the final period of human history is now upon the world. Throughout Revelation, the concept of judgment plays a central role, as God's righteous judgment is poured out upon a world that has largely rejected Him and embraced evil.

The announcement of judgment here is both a warning and a call to action. It serves as a final wake-up call to those who have not yet turned to God, urging them to repent before it is too late. The angel's message is clear: the window of opportunity for repentance is closing rapidly, and those who continue to resist God's call will soon face the full consequences of their rebellion.

For Christians, the announcement of the "hour of judgment" is also a reminder that God's justice will ultimately prevail. Despite the suffering and persecution that believers may endure, they are reassured that God will set things right. The evils of the world, represented by the beast, Babylon, and other symbols of corruption in Revelation, will not go unpunished. God's judgment is both a necessary and righteous act to cleanse the world of sin and to establish His eternal kingdom.

The Universality of the Gospel Message

One of the most striking aspects of the first angel's message is its universal scope. The angel is seen "flying in midair," a position that indicates the visibility and reach of the message. This gospel is proclaimed to "every nation, tribe, tongue, and people" (Revelation 14:6), highlighting that it is a message for all of humanity. No group is excluded from hearing this final call to repentance and worship.

This universal scope reflects the inclusive nature of the gospel message. God's offer of salvation is not limited to a specific ethnic group, culture, or nation; it is extended to all people. This echoes the words of Jesus in the Great Commission: "Go therefore and make disciples of all nations" (Matthew 28:19). The angel's proclamation reinforces the idea that the gospel must reach the ends of the earth before the final judgment comes.

The global nature of this proclamation also emphasizes the accountability of all humanity. No one will be able to claim ignorance of the message. The angel's proclamation reaches every corner of the earth, making clear that every individual must make a decision in response to the gospel. The message of salvation is available to all, but each person must choose whether to accept or reject it.

The Final Call to Repentance

The first angel's proclamation represents the final opportunity for humanity to turn to God before the judgment is fully unleashed. In many ways, this message is the culmination of God's ongoing efforts to call people to repentance throughout history. From the prophets of the Old Testament to the ministry of Jesus and the apostles, God has continually extended an invitation to humanity to return to Him and receive His grace.

Yet the urgency of the angel's message reminds us that time is running out. The "hour of His judgment" is no longer in the distant future; it has arrived. For those who have resisted or delayed responding to God's call, this message is a clear warning that the time for decision is now. There is no more room for complacency or indifference.

For Christians, the first angel's message also serves as a reminder of the importance of evangelism. As followers of Christ, believers are called to share the gospel with those who have not yet heard it or responded to it. In the final days before God's judgment, the task of proclaiming the good news takes on even greater urgency. The message of the everlasting gospel is one of hope, but it must be shared before the time for repentance is gone.

Spiritual Application

The message of the first angel has several important spiritual applications for Christians today:

1. Worship God Alone: The angel's call to "fear God and give Him glory" challenges believers to examine their own lives and ensure that their worship is directed to God alone. In a world filled with distractions, false idols, and competing allegiances, Christians must be vigilant in maintaining their devotion to the Creator. This includes rejecting the temptations of materialism, power, and self-glorification that the world often offers.

2. Reverence for God's Judgment: The announcement that "the hour of His judgment has come" reminds believers that God's judgment is imminent. While this can be a sobering thought, it also serves as a reminder that God's justice will prevail, and His righteousness will be fully revealed. For Christians, this should inspire a sense of urgency in living out their faith and sharing the gospel with others.

3. Proclaiming the Gospel: Just as the first angel proclaims the everlasting gospel to all nations, believers today are called to share the good news of salvation with the world.

The universality of the gospel reminds us that no one is beyond the reach of God's grace, and Christians have a responsibility to ensure that the message is shared far and wide.

4. Living with Urgency: The angel's message reminds us that the time for repentance is limited. Christians are called to live with a sense of urgency, knowing that the return of Christ and the final judgment could come at any time. This urgency should motivate believers to live faithfully, proclaim the gospel, and prioritize what truly matters in light of eternity.

The first angel's proclamation of the everlasting gospel in Revelation 14 is a powerful reminder of God's offer of salvation and the imminence of His judgment. It is a final call for all of humanity to turn to God, worship the Creator, and repent before it is too late. The message is both one of hope and a solemn warning, underscoring the need for immediate action in response to God's grace.

For Christians, the first angel's message serves as a call to worship God faithfully, to share the gospel with urgency, and to live with an awareness of the coming judgment. As we await the fulfillment of God's plan, we are reminded that the gospel is everlasting, and it remains the foundation of our hope, even in the face of the trials and challenges that lie ahead.

The Second Angel - The Fall of Babylon

In Revelation 14:8, the second angel appears, following the first angel's proclamation of the everlasting gospel, to deliver a simple but powerful message: "Babylon is fallen, is fallen, that great city, because she has made all nations drink of the wine of the wrath of her fornication." This declaration is profound and serves as a prophetic announcement of the impending destruction of Babylon, a symbol representing the corrupt system of the world that stands in opposition to God. The fall of Babylon signifies the inevitable collapse of all human systems of power, idolatry, and rebellion against God.

This message, although brief, carries immense theological and symbolic weight. It serves as a warning and a reassurance—a warning to those who continue to align themselves with the corrupt world system symbolized by Babylon, and a reassurance to believers that no worldly power, no matter how formidable, can withstand the judgment of God. This proclamation of Babylon's fall echoes throughout the book of Revelation and points toward the ultimate victory of God's kingdom over all earthly powers that oppose Him.

Babylon: Symbol of Corruption and Rebellion

In the Bible, Babylon is not just a city, but a symbol of human pride, rebellion, and opposition to God. Historically, Babylon was a powerful empire known for its wealth, grandeur, and idolatry. It was the nation that destroyed Jerusalem and took the Israelites into captivity. The city of Babylon became a symbol of arrogance, immorality, and opposition to God's people. Its fall, prophesied in the Old Testament, marked the end of a system that defied God's authority and sought to exalt itself above Him (Isaiah 13-14, Jeremiah 50-51).

In Revelation, Babylon takes on an even more significant symbolic role. It represents the entire system of the world that is in rebellion against God—a system characterized by spiritual adultery, idolatry, materialism, and injustice. Babylon stands as the epitome of worldly power and influence, drawing nations and peoples into its corruption. It is described as a place of "fornication", a metaphor for the spiritual adultery and idolatry that leads people away from true worship of God.

The angel's declaration that "Babylon is fallen" is a prophetic announcement of the downfall of this corrupt system. Just as ancient Babylon was overthrown, the spiritual Babylon—symbolizing all human power structures that reject God—will also fall. This fall is inevitable because it is a part of God's final judgment against sin and evil in the world. The repetition of "is fallen, is fallen" emphasizes the certainty and finality of this judgment.

The Corrupting Influence of Babylon

The angel goes on to say that Babylon has "made all nations drink of the wine of the wrath of her fornication" (Revelation 14:8). This statement highlights the corrupting influence that Babylon has had on the world. The imagery of wine often symbolizes intoxication or influence in the Bible. Here, Babylon's wine represents the enticements and seductions of the world—its wealth, power, immorality, and idolatry. Nations and peoples have been lured into a spiritual stupor, forsaking God and indulging in the sinful pleasures and ambitions that Babylon offers.

The phrase "the wine of the wrath of her fornication" also suggests that Babylon's actions have provoked God's wrath. Her spiritual adultery—leading people into idolatry and rebellion—has reached its fullness, and now she is ripe for judgment. The nations that have participated in Babylon's corruption are not merely victims; they have willingly drunk from her cup, sharing in her sins and, ultimately, in her judgment.

This message serves as a warning to all who align themselves with the world's systems of power, wealth, and corruption. Babylon's fall is not just the collapse of a city but the downfall of everything that opposes God. Those who have participated in her immorality will share in her punishment unless they repent and turn to God.

The Fall of Earthly Powers

The fall of Babylon represents the collapse of all human institutions and powers that have exalted themselves above God. Throughout history, empires and nations have risen to great heights, often through exploitation, immorality, and idolatry. These powers, though they may seem invincible at the height of their glory, are ultimately subject to the judgment of God. No earthly power, no matter how mighty, can stand against His justice.

In this sense, Babylon represents not just a single empire or nation but the entire system of human rebellion against God. It symbolizes the corrupt institutions, ideologies, and cultures that lead people away from true worship and into a life of spiritual adultery. This includes not only political and economic systems but also cultural and religious structures that reject God's authority and promote false worship.

The fall of Babylon is a reminder that all worldly systems—no matter how powerful or enduring they may appear—are temporary. They will all eventually fall before the righteous judgment of God. This is a message of hope for believers, especially those who suffer under corrupt governments, oppressive systems, or unjust institutions. The fall of Babylon assures them that God is in control, and He will bring justice to the world.

A Message of Judgment and Hope

The proclamation of Babylon's fall is both a message of judgment and a message of hope. For those who have placed their trust in the world and its corrupt systems, it is a message of judgment. Babylon's fall means the collapse of everything they have depended on for security, power, and identity. It signals the end of their way of life, which has been built on idolatry, immorality, and rebellion.

For believers, however, the fall of Babylon is a message of hope. It assures them that the corrupt systems of the world will not last forever. The forces that oppose God and oppress His people will be overthrown, and His kingdom will be established in their place. The fall of Babylon is the beginning of the ultimate triumph of God's kingdom, where justice, righteousness, and true worship will prevail.

This dual message of judgment and hope is central to the book of Revelation. The fall of Babylon is not merely an isolated event but part of the larger narrative of God's redemptive plan. It signifies the end of the old, corrupt world order and the beginning of the new heavens and new earth, where God will reign in glory and His people will dwell with Him forever.

The Symbolism of Babylon in Revelation

The symbolism of Babylon in Revelation is further developed in later chapters, particularly in Revelation 17 and 18. In these chapters, Babylon is depicted as a "great prostitute", riding on the beast, adorned with wealth, and drunk on the blood of the saints. This imagery highlights the depth of Babylon's corruption and her involvement in persecuting God's people. Babylon represents not just a political or economic system but a spiritual force that leads people away from God and into idolatry.

In Revelation 18, the fall of Babylon is described in detail, with merchants and kings mourning her destruction because their wealth and power were tied to her prosperity. The fall of Babylon is portrayed as sudden and catastrophic, emphasizing that God's judgment is swift and final. The imagery of Babylon's destruction serves as a stark reminder that no matter how powerful the world's systems may appear, they are fragile in the face of God's sovereignty.

For believers, the fall of Babylon in Revelation is a call to remain separate from the world's corrupt systems. In Revelation 18:4, a voice from heaven calls out, "Come out of her, my people, so that you will not share in her sins, so that you will not receive any of her plagues." This is a call to spiritual purity and to reject the seductions of the world that lead to compromise and unfaithfulness to God.

Spiritual Application

The fall of Babylon in Revelation 14:8 holds profound spiritual implications for Christians today:

1. Rejecting Worldly Systems: Babylon symbolizes the corrupt systems of power, wealth, and influence that lead people away from God. Believers are called to reject these systems and not be enticed by their false promises of security and success. The fall of Babylon reminds Christians that all worldly powers and institutions will ultimately fall before God's judgment.

2. Spiritual Adultery: The angel's message about Babylon's "fornication" highlights the danger of spiritual adultery—turning away from God to pursue false idols, whether they be material wealth, power, or personal ambition. Christians are called to remain faithful to God, resisting the temptation to compromise their faith for worldly gain.

3. The Inevitability of God's Judgment: The fall of Babylon serves as a reminder that God's judgment is inevitable and righteous. No matter how secure or powerful the systems of the world may seem, they cannot stand against the sovereignty of God. This truth gives believers hope in the

face of injustice and oppression, knowing that God will bring justice in His time.

4. Living with an Eternal Perspective: The fall of Babylon encourages Christians to live with an eternal perspective, recognizing that the things of this world are temporary and fleeting. Believers are called to invest their lives in

God's kingdom, which is eternal and will never fall. This perspective helps Christians to endure trials, knowing that the kingdom of God will ultimately prevail.

The proclamation of the second angel that "Babylon is fallen" serves as a powerful declaration of the inevitable downfall of the corrupt systems of the world that stand in opposition to God. Babylon represents more than just a city; it is a symbol of human rebellion, idolatry, and spiritual adultery. Its fall is a reminder that no earthly power or institution can withstand the judgment of God.

For believers, this message offers both a warning and a hope. It warns against aligning with the world's corrupt systems and participating in its idolatry. At the same time, it provides hope that God's kingdom will prevail, and all who remain faithful to Him will share in His victory. The fall of Babylon is the beginning of the end of the old world order and the ushering in of God's eternal reign of righteousness and justice.

The Third Angel – The Warning Against the Beast

In Revelation 14:9-11, the third angel follows the proclamations of the first two angels, delivering a severe and urgent warning: "If anyone worships the beast and its image and receives its mark on their forehead or on their hand, they too will drink the wine of God's fury, which has been poured full strength into the cup of his wrath." This message serves as a solemn reminder of the consequences of aligning with the forces of evil and opposition to God. Those who worship the beast or bear its mark will face the full measure of God's judgment.

The third angel's message is the most direct and frightening of the three angelic proclamations. While the first angel extends a call to worship God, and the second declares the fall of Babylon, the third angel offers a stark and uncompromising warning to those who choose to align themselves with the beast and its corrupt system. This passage challenges believers to stand firm in their allegiance to God, even in the face of persecution or pressure to conform, knowing that the eternal consequences of worshiping the beast are devastating.

The Beast and Its Mark: Symbols of Evil and Rebellion

In order to understand the third angel's warning, it is important to revisit the symbolic significance of the beast and its mark. Earlier in Revelation, the beast is introduced as a representation of evil, specifically the anti-God powers that dominate the world and lead people away from true worship. In Revelation 13, the beast rises from the sea and exercises authority over the earth, demanding worship from all who dwell on the earth. The false prophet (the second beast) works alongside the first beast to deceive people into worshiping the beast's image and receiving its mark on their foreheads or hands (Revelation 13:11-18).

The mark of the beast is not simply a physical mark but symbolizes allegiance to the beast's system—a system of idolatry, immorality, and rebellion against God. Those who receive the mark are those who willingly submit to the beast's authority and reject the sovereignty of God. The mark represents a choice between two kingdoms: the kingdom of the beast, which is opposed to God, and the kingdom of Christ. It signifies a deliberate decision to reject God and embrace the evil system that the beast represents.

In the third angel's warning, those who worship the beast and receive its mark are condemned to face the wrath of God. The mark of the beast is in direct contrast to the seal of God given to the 144,000 in Revelation 7, which represents divine protection and belonging to God. While the mark of the beast leads to judgment, the seal of God guarantees salvation. This stark contrast emphasizes the spiritual choices that humanity must make: to follow God or to follow the beast.

The Consequences of Worshiping the Beast

The third angel's message is clear: those who worship the beast and receive its mark will face the full and terrifying wrath of God. The imagery used in this warning is intense and emphasizes the seriousness of the consequences. The angel declares that they will "drink the wine of God's fury, which has been poured full strength into the cup of His wrath" (Revelation 14:10). This metaphor of drinking the wine of God's wrath is drawn from the Old Testament, where the cup of wrath represents divine judgment upon nations or individuals who oppose God (Jeremiah 25:15-17, Isaiah 51:17).

In biblical times, wine was often diluted with water to make it less potent, but the wine of God's wrath is described as being poured full strength, meaning it is undiluted and extremely powerful. This imagery conveys the severity and totality of God's judgment against those who have chosen to align with the beast. There will be no escape or mitigation for those who have worshiped the beast—they will experience God's judgment in its fullest measure.

The consequences of worshiping the beast are further described as eternal torment. The angel declares that those who receive the mark of the beast will be "tormented with burning sulfur in the presence of the holy angels and of the Lamb. And the smoke of their torment will rise forever and ever" (Revelation 14:10-11). This vivid and disturbing imagery points to the eternal consequences of rejecting God. The torment is not temporary but everlasting, indicating that the judgment for those who worship the beast is permanent.

The presence of the holy angels and the Lamb during this judgment emphasizes the justice and righteousness of God's wrath. The Lamb, who is Jesus Christ, oversees the final judgment, ensuring that it is just and deserved. The smoke rising forever and ever symbolizes the unending nature of this punishment, highlighting the eternal ramifications of the decision to worship the beast.

The Warning to Remain Faithful

The third angel's warning is not only a message of judgment but also serves as a call to faithfulness. The frightening consequences of worshiping the beast are presented as a stark contrast to the reward of those who remain loyal to God. The severity of this warning is intended to shake people out of complacency and urge them to consider the eternal consequences of their choices.

In Revelation 14:12, the focus shifts briefly to offer encouragement to the saints: "Here is the patience of the saints; here are those who keep the commandments of God and the faith of Jesus." This verse serves as an exhortation to believers to remain faithful to God, even in the face of persecution and the temptation to compromise. The saints are described as those who patiently endure and hold fast to their faith in Jesus, despite the pressures and threats from the beast's system.

This call to perseverance is especially significant in the context of the broader narrative of Revelation, where Christians are frequently depicted as suffering under the persecution of the beast and the false prophet. The temptation to worship the beast or receive its mark may come with the promise of economic security, social acceptance, or even survival, but the third angel's message reminds believers that such compromise will ultimately lead to destruction.

The choice for Christians is clear: they must remain faithful to God and resist the temptations of the beast, even if it means facing persecution, economic hardship, or death. The rewards for endurance are described earlier in Revelation, where those who remain faithful are promised to stand with the Lamb on Mount Zion and share in His eternal kingdom (Revelation 14:1-5).

The Importance of Spiritual Discernment

One of the key themes of the third angel's message is the importance of spiritual discernment. The mark of the beast is not just a literal symbol but represents the broader spiritual decision to align with the forces of evil or with God. In a world where the beast's influence is pervasive—manifesting in political, economic, social, and even religious systems—believers must exercise discernment to recognize and reject these false systems of power.

The call to reject the mark of the beast is a call to resist the cultural, political, and spiritual pressures that lead people away from God. In every generation, the beast can be understood as the various systems and powers that demand allegiance in ways that are contrary to the gospel. These powers seduce people with promises of security, success, and prosperity, but they ultimately lead to spiritual death.

Believers must remain vigilant, discerning the difference between worldly power and God's kingdom. The mark of the beast is a reminder that every Christian is faced with the decision of where to place their allegiance—whether to follow the ways of the world or to remain faithful to God, no matter the cost.

Spiritual Application

The third angel's warning against worshiping the beast and receiving its mark holds deep spiritual implications for Christians today:

1. Allegiance to God Alone: The warning against receiving the mark of the beast challenges believers to examine where their allegiance lies. Christians are called to be faithful to God alone, resisting any pressures—whether social, political, or economic—that would cause them to compromise their faith. The call to worship God, rather than the beast, is a call to radical loyalty to Christ, even in the face of persecution or hardship.

2. The Consequences of Compromise: The third angel's message underscores the seriousness of spiritual compromise. Those who choose to worship the beast or receive its mark may do so out of fear, convenience, or the desire for acceptance, but the eternal consequences are devastating. This message serves as a reminder that even small compromises in faith can lead to a rejection of God's sovereignty and, ultimately, to judgment.

3. Perseverance in Faith: The exhortation to persevere is central to the message of Revelation. The third angel's warning encourages believers to endure, knowing that their

faithfulness will be rewarded. Even in the face of persecution or hardship, Christians are called to hold fast to their faith in Jesus, trusting that God will bring justice and vindication in the end.

4. Eternal Consequences: The vivid imagery of eternal torment and the cup of God's wrath reminds believers of the eternal nature of spiritual decisions. The choice to follow Christ or to follow the beast is not merely a temporary decision; it has eternal ramifications. This truth should motivate Christians to live with an awareness of eternity, making decisions that honor God and reflect their loyalty to Him.

5. Spiritual Discernment: In a world filled with false systems of power and deception, the third angel's message challenges believers to exercise spiritual discernment. Christians must recognize the ways in which the beast's influence is present in today's world—whether through political, economic, or cultural systems—and resist the temptation to conform. Instead, they are called to live counterculturally, with their eyes fixed on God's kingdom.

The third angel's warning in Revelation 14:9-11 serves as a powerful and sobering reminder of the eternal consequences of worshiping the beast and receiving its mark. Those who align themselves with the forces of evil and opposition to God will face the full wrath of God's judgment, experiencing eternal torment and separation from God. This stark warning is a call to remain faithful to God, even in the face of persecution and temptation.

For believers, the third angel's message is both a warning and an encouragement. It warns of the consequences of compromise and the eternal nature of spiritual decisions, while also encouraging Christians to persevere in their faith and remain loyal to God, no matter the cost. In a world filled with false allegiances and competing powers, the call to worship God alone and reject the influence of the beast remains as relevant today as it was in John's time.

Spiritual Application

The messages of the three angels in Revelation 14:6-13 serve as a profound and urgent reminder to humanity of the spiritual realities we face in the final days. Together, these messages emphasize the urgency of the gospel, the necessity of repentance, the certainty of judgment, and the promise of salvation for those who remain faithful to God. As Christians reflect on these angelic proclamations, they are called to live with a greater sense of eternity in mind, knowing that the present world is temporary and that their ultimate hope lies in God's eternal kingdom.

1. The Urgency of the Gospel

The proclamation of the first angel highlights the urgency of the gospel message. The angel carries the everlasting gospel to all nations, tribes, tongues, and people, offering humanity one final opportunity to repent and turn to God before the coming judgment. This message emphasizes that the gospel is not just an ancient truth, but an eternal one—the good news of salvation has always been and will always be the path to reconciliation with God.

For Christians, this first message serves as a call to urgency in sharing the gospel. The angel's proclamation is a reminder that time is running out for those who have not yet repented. As believers, we are entrusted with the mission to share the gospel with others before the final judgment arrives. This requires us to approach evangelism with a renewed sense of purpose and passion, knowing that God desires all people to hear the message of salvation and turn to Him.

The gospel message also reminds us of the centrality of worshiping God as the Creator. In a world filled with distractions and competing ideologies, the angel's call to "fear God and give Him glory" is a reminder to prioritize our worship and reverence for God above all else. The angel's warning that "the hour of His judgment has come" compels believers to align their lives with God's purposes and to lead others to recognize the importance of worshiping Him alone.

2. The Call to Repentance

The second angel declares the fall of Babylon, symbolizing the collapse of all corrupt and idolatrous systems that oppose God. Babylon represents the world's rebellion, idolatry, and pursuit of material wealth and pleasure at the expense of spiritual truth. The angel's message highlights the inevitable judgment on all worldly systems that are built on sin and pride.

For believers, this is a clear call to repentance. We are reminded that no matter how powerful or alluring the systems of the world may seem, they are destined for destruction. The fall of Babylon challenges us to evaluate our own lives and to reject the idols—whether they be wealth, power, or personal ambition—that seek to draw us away from our loyalty to God. Christians are called to remain spiritually pure, resisting the temptations of the world and living in a way that reflects their allegiance to Christ, not to Babylon.

The angel's message also serves as a warning to repent of any compromise with the world's values. For those who have been seduced by the allure of Babylon, there is still time to turn back to God and escape the judgment that is coming upon the world. This message urges us to remain vigilant, ensuring that our faith is not corrupted by the influence of the world, but remains rooted in the truth of God's Word.

3. The Certainty of Judgment

The third angel delivers the most severe message, warning against worshiping the beast and receiving its mark. This message emphasizes the eternal consequences of aligning oneself with the forces of evil and rebellion against God. Those who worship the beast and receive its mark will face the full wrath of God—a judgment that results in eternal torment and separation from God.

For Christians, this serves as a powerful reminder of the certainty of God's judgment. The third angel's warning underscores the reality that every person must make a choice: to either follow Christ or to follow the beast, which symbolizes the forces of evil and rebellion in the world. There is no middle ground, and the consequences of this choice are eternal. This should instill in us a reverent fear of God and a recognition that our decisions in this life have eternal implications.

The image of eternal torment described in this passage challenges us to reflect on the seriousness of rejecting God and His offer of salvation. While the gospel is a message of hope, it is also a message of accountability. God's judgment is just and righteous, and those who choose to rebel against Him will face the consequences of their choices. As Christians, this reality should motivate us to live lives that are pleasing to God and to share the gospel with urgency, knowing that people's eternal destinies are at stake.

4. The Promise of Salvation for the Faithful

While the messages of the three angels are filled with warnings of judgment, they also carry a promise of salvation for those who remain faithful to God. In Revelation 14:12, following the third angel's message, there is an encouragement for the saints: "Here is the patience of the saints; here are those who keep the commandments of God and the faith of Jesus." This call to endurance is a reminder that believers are called to remain faithful in the face of persecution, temptation, and pressure to conform to the world's systems.

For Christians, this promise of salvation is both a comfort and a challenge. We are comforted by the knowledge that those who remain faithful to God will be vindicated and rewarded in the end. Even in the midst of trials and tribulations, we can take heart knowing that God sees our perseverance and that we will share in His ultimate victory.

At the same time, this call to faithfulness challenges us to endure the difficulties of life with patience and trust in God. The forces of the world, symbolized by the beast and Babylon, may seem overwhelming at times, but believers are encouraged to remain steadfast, knowing that God's kingdom will prevail. This perseverance is not a passive waiting but an active commitment to living out our faith, keeping God's commandments, and holding fast to the testimony of Jesus, no matter the cost.

5. Living with an Eternal Perspective

The overarching theme of the three angelic messages is the call for Christians to live with an eternal perspective. The world we live in is temporary, and everything associated with the systems of the beast and Babylon will ultimately pass away. The fall of Babylon and the judgment of the beast serve as a reminder that our true hope lies not in the things of this world but in the eternal kingdom of God.

Living with an eternal perspective means that we are called to prioritize the things that last—our relationship with God, our faith, and our obedience to His Word. It means rejecting the fleeting pleasures and temptations of the world, knowing that they will lead to destruction, and instead focusing on building our lives on the foundation of Christ, which is unshakable.

This eternal perspective also helps us to endure suffering and persecution with hope. Just as the saints are encouraged to remain faithful in the face of trials, Christians today can find strength in knowing that their ultimate reward is with God in eternity. The world may offer temporary pleasures, but the joy and peace of God's kingdom are eternal.

The spiritual application of the three angelic messages in Revelation 14 emphasizes the urgency of the gospel, the necessity of repentance, the certainty of judgment, and the promise of salvation for those who remain faithful. Christians are called to live with an eternal perspective, recognizing that the world we know is temporary and that only those who trust in God and follow Him will stand in the end.

As we reflect on these messages, we are reminded to live with urgency in sharing the gospel, to repent of any spiritual compromise, and to persevere in our faith no matter the challenges we face. The angels' warnings of judgment should motivate us to remain loyal to God and to lead others to the saving knowledge of Christ, knowing that the time for repentance is limited and that the eternal kingdom of God is at hand.

CHAPTER 03

THE PATIENCE AND ENDURANCE OF THE SAINTS

In Revelation 14:12-13, after the proclamations of the three angels warning of impending judgment, we encounter a brief yet powerful pause. This moment serves as a word of encouragement to the faithful believers who are enduring persecution, temptation, and hardship. The message is clear: "Here is the patience of the saints; here are those who keep the commandments of God and the faith of Jesus."

These verses emphasize the importance of patience and endurance for those who remain loyal to God in the face of tribulation. Believers are called to hold fast to their faith in Christ and remain obedient to God's commandments, even when the forces of evil, symbolized by the beast and Babylon, seem overwhelming. This passage serves as a reminder that the trials of this world are temporary, but the reward for faithful endurance is eternal.

The Call to Patience and Endurance

The word patience in this context refers to steadfastness, perseverance, or endurance under pressure. In Revelation, the saints are depicted as those who faithfully follow Christ, even when it requires suffering. Their patience is not passive but active—it is the strength to endure tribulation while maintaining faith in God and obedience to His commands.

Throughout the Book of Revelation, believers are repeatedly called to persevere in their faith. The world they inhabit is dominated by corrupt systems of power, symbolized by the beast and Babylon, which tempt or coerce people to abandon their loyalty to God. Despite these challenges, the saints are exhorted to remain firm, trusting that God's righteous judgment is coming and that their perseverance will be rewarded.

In Revelation 14, the earlier warnings of judgment—especially the eternal consequences of worshiping the beast and receiving its mark—are not only for those who rebel against God but also serve as a means of encouraging believers to remain steadfast. The saints are those who choose to follow Christ rather than conforming to the world, even at great personal cost. They resist the beast's system of oppression and false worship, knowing that their allegiance is to God alone.

The endurance of the saints is not just a matter of passive waiting for deliverance. It is an active, faithful endurance—a life characterized by obedience to God's commandments and unwavering faith in Jesus. The phrase "the patience of the saints" reflects their strength and resolve to stand firm, even when persecuted, knowing that God's ultimate victory is assured.

Keeping the Commandments of God and the Faith of Jesus

The passage describes the saints as those who "keep the commandments of God and the faith of Jesus." This description highlights two key aspects of Christian life: obedience and faith.

- Obedience to the Commandments of God: The saints are marked by their commitment to following God's laws and instructions. In a world that often rejects or distorts God's moral order, these believers choose to live in accordance with His will. Obedience to God's commandments is an outward expression of their allegiance to Him, demonstrating that they have not been seduced by the corrupt systems of the world.

This obedience is not legalistic; rather, it flows from a heart that seeks to honor God in all things. The commandments of God are not burdensome to them but are the natural response of those who love and follow Him. In keeping God's commandments, the saints bear witness to their trust in His sovereignty and their desire to live according to His kingdom values.

- Faith in Jesus: The saints are also characterized by their faith in Jesus—a deep, abiding trust in Christ as their Lord and Savior. This faith is not merely intellectual assent but a living faith that shapes every aspect of their lives. Despite the opposition and persecution they face, the saints hold fast to their faith in Christ, trusting in His promise of eternal life and His ultimate victory over evil.

The faith of the saints is especially significant in the context of Revelation, where they are constantly pressured to abandon their allegiance to Christ and worship the beast. Their refusal to compromise, even under threat of death, is a testament to the strength of their faith. They know that their hope is in Christ alone, and they are willing to endure suffering for His sake, trusting that He will reward their faithfulness in the end.

The Blessing of the Faithful Dead

In Revelation 14:13, John hears a voice from heaven proclaiming a blessing: "Blessed are the dead who die in the Lord from now on." This blessing is a word of comfort to those who face martyrdom or death because of their faith in Christ. It reassures believers that their death in the Lord is not in vain but will be followed by eternal rest and reward.

The voice continues, "Yes," says the Spirit, "they will rest from their labors, for their deeds will follow them." This promise of rest is significant, as it speaks to the ultimate peace and joy that awaits those who have endured faithfully. While they may have suffered greatly in this life, they will experience eternal rest in the presence of God. Their "labors" refer to their acts of faith, their obedience, and their perseverance, all of which will be remembered and rewarded by God.

This blessing also emphasizes that death is not the end for those who "die in the Lord." While physical death may come as a result of persecution or martyrdom, it is followed by eternal life in God's presence. The promise of rest and reward encourages believers to remain steadfast in their faith, knowing that their suffering will not be forgotten, and they will ultimately share in Christ's victory.

The phrase "their deeds will follow them" underscores the idea that the faithful works of the saints have eternal significance. Though their suffering and faithfulness may not be recognized or rewarded in this life, God sees their deeds, and they will be vindicated and rewarded in the life to come. This promise is a source of great comfort for believers who may feel overwhelmed by the challenges of this world, as it reassures them that their faithfulness will not go unnoticed by God.

Spiritual Application

The patience and endurance of the saints in Revelation 14:12-13 provides several key spiritual applications for Christians today:

1. Persevering in Faith: Believers are called to persevere in their faith, even in the face of trials, persecution, or pressure to conform to the world. The saints are those who remain loyal to God, refusing to compromise with the corrupt systems of the world. This endurance is not a passive waiting but an active commitment to live in obedience to God and to trust in Christ's promises, no matter the cost.

2. Obedience to God's Commandments: Obedience is a mark of the faithful. In a world that often rejects God's moral order, Christians are called to live in alignment with God's will, keeping His commandments as an expression of their devotion to Him. This obedience is not driven by fear or legalism but by love for God and a desire to honor Him.

3. Trusting in Jesus: The faith of the saints is a deep and abiding trust in Christ, even when circumstances are

difficult. Christians are called to hold fast to their faith in Jesus, trusting that He will ultimately bring justice and reward to those who endure. In a world filled with uncertainty and temptation, believers must continually anchor their hope in Christ and His eternal promises.

4. Living with an Eternal Perspective: The promise of rest and reward for those who die in the Lord reminds Christians to live with an eternal perspective. While the trials and challenges of this life may be difficult, they are temporary. The reward for faithful endurance is eternal rest in the presence of God. This perspective helps believers to endure hardship, knowing that their suffering is not in vain and that their deeds will be remembered by God.

5. Hope for the Faithful Dead: The blessing pronounced on those who die in the Lord offers hope and comfort to believers, especially those facing persecution or death for their faith. Death is not the end for the saints; it is the beginning of eternal life with God. The promise of rest and reward encourages believers to face death with confidence and hope, knowing that they will be vindicated and that their faithfulness will be rewarded.

The patience and endurance of the saints in Revelation 14:12-13 serves as a powerful reminder for Christians to remain faithful, obedient, and steadfast in the face of tribulation and hardship. The call to keep the commandments of God and hold fast to the faith of Jesus is central to the life of every believer. No matter the challenges they face, Christians are encouraged to persevere, trusting that their endurance will be rewarded with eternal rest and divine recognition.

The blessing pronounced on those who "die in the Lord" offers a message of hope and assurance. Even in the face of death, those who remain faithful to God will find rest from their labors and be rewarded for their deeds. This passage invites believers to live with an eternal perspective, knowing that the trials of this life are temporary, but the reward for faithfulness is eternal.

Patience and Endurance

In Revelation 14:12-13, after a series of dire warnings and proclamations of impending judgment, a moment of encouragement is offered to the faithful believers. These verses focus on the essential qualities that will carry Christians through the trials of the end times: patience and endurance. The saints are called to maintain their faith and obedience to God even in the face of extreme adversity. Their perseverance is a demonstration of their loyalty to Christ, and it is this steadfast faith that will lead to their ultimate victory.

Endurance in the Face of Trials

The saints are called to endurance, a quality that is indispensable in the midst of the severe trials and tribulations that define the end times. The world described in the Book of Revelation is one of immense pressure, with believers facing persecution, temptation, and threats from the forces of evil, represented by the beast and Babylon. Despite these challenges, the saints are called to hold fast to their faith in God and to remain obedient to His commandments.

Endurance, in this context, is not simply the act of waiting out difficult times, but rather a form of active perseverance. It requires an intentional and continuous commitment to following God's ways, even when everything in the world seems to be falling apart. This endurance involves standing firm in faith, not allowing circumstances to weaken one's resolve or lead to spiritual compromise.

The trials of the end times, as described in Revelation, may come in the form of persecution, social pressure to conform to the worship of the beast, or economic hardship. In the face of these overwhelming challenges, the saints are encouraged to persevere, trusting that their faithfulness will ultimately be rewarded by God. The patience required is one that anticipates God's final judgment, where justice will be served, and His kingdom will be fully established.

Faithfulness to God's Commandments

One of the defining characteristics of the saints is their obedience to God's commandments. In Revelation 14:12, they are described as those who "keep the commandments of God". This faithfulness is essential in distinguishing the saints from those who follow the beast. While the world around them may be crumbling under the influence of corruption and idolatry, the saints remain committed to living according to God's standards.

Obedience to God's commandments reflects the saints' loyalty to His kingdom and their refusal to bow to the demands of the beast or the corrupt systems of Babylon. This obedience is not legalistic but arises from a deep love for God and a desire to honor Him in all aspects of life. Even in the face of great temptation, the saints continue to walk in the ways of righteousness, trusting that God's commandments lead to life, whereas the way of the beast leads to destruction.

The call to keep the commandments of God in the midst of tribulation is a reminder that faith is not just an inward belief but is expressed through one's actions and choices. It is through this obedience that the saints bear witness to their allegiance to God, and their lives become a testimony to the power of faith in Jesus Christ.

The Faith of Jesus

The endurance of the saints is also tied to their faith in Jesus. In addition to keeping God's commandments, the saints are described as holding fast to their faith in Jesus (Revelation 14:12). This faith is not simply a passive trust, but an active and living faith that perseveres through trials. It involves a deep, personal relationship with Christ, characterized by trust, loyalty, and a willingness to suffer for His name.

Faith in Jesus means trusting in His promises, even when circumstances suggest otherwise. During the end times, when the world is dominated by the beast's power and believers face persecution, the temptation to abandon one's faith may be strong. However, the saints remain steadfast, clinging to the truth that Jesus has already won the victory through His death and resurrection and that His kingdom will ultimately prevail.

Their faith in Jesus also gives them strength to endure the hardships they face. Just as Christ Himself endured suffering for the sake of humanity, so too are the saints called to endure for the sake of the gospel. This faith enables them to look beyond the present difficulties and fix their eyes on the eternal hope that awaits them in God's kingdom.

Active Endurance: A Call to Action

The endurance that the saints are called to is not passive waiting but an active commitment to God's truth in the midst of adversity. This kind of endurance requires constant vigilance and spiritual strength. It means continually choosing to follow Christ, even when it would be easier to give in to the pressures of the world.

The saints are engaged in a spiritual battle against the forces of evil. Their endurance is an act of resistance against the corruption and idolatry that the beast represents. It involves actively rejecting the mark of the beast, which symbolizes allegiance to the world's corrupt systems, and instead embracing the seal of God, which marks them as His faithful people.

Endurance is also about standing firm in one's convictions. In the face of persecution or even death, the saints do not waver. They remain committed to their faith, knowing that their ultimate victory is assured in Christ. Their endurance is motivated by their knowledge that God's justice will prevail, and that those who remain faithful will share in the triumph of His kingdom.

Ultimate Victory through Endurance

The patience and endurance of the saints will ultimately lead to their victory. While the trials they face in the present may seem overwhelming, they know that their faithfulness will be rewarded. Revelation 14:13 offers a word of comfort and hope: "Blessed are the dead who die in the Lord from now on… they will rest from their labors, for their deeds will follow them."

This blessing underscores the eternal reward for those who endure in faith. Even death cannot separate the saints from the victory that is promised to them in Christ. They will find rest from their labors, meaning that the trials and hardships they have endured will give way to eternal peace and joy in the presence of God. Moreover, their deeds will follow them, indicating that their faithfulness in life will be remembered and rewarded in eternity.

This assurance of victory gives the saints the strength to continue their faithful endurance. They know that the trials they face are temporary, but the reward for their perseverance is eternal. In the end, their faithfulness will be vindicated, and they will share in the joy of Christ's triumph over evil.

Spiritual Application

The call to endurance in Revelation 14:12-13 provides several important spiritual applications for Christians today:

1. Enduring through Trials: Just as the saints are called to endure the trials of the end times, Christians today are encouraged to persevere through the challenges they face. Whether it be personal suffering, persecution, or societal pressures to compromise, believers must remain committed

to their faith, knowing that their endurance will lead to victory in Christ.

2. Obedience to God's Commandments: The saints are described as those who keep God's commandments, and this is a reminder for Christians to live lives of obedience to God. Even in a world that often rejects or distorts God's moral order, believers are called to stand firm in their commitment to righteousness and to follow God's ways.

3. Active Faith: Endurance is not passive but requires active faith. Christians are called to be vigilant in their walk with God, resisting the temptations and pressures of the world and choosing to remain loyal to Christ, even when it is difficult.

4. Trusting in Christ's Victory: The endurance of the saints is rooted in their faith in Jesus. Christians can take comfort in knowing that, despite the trials they may face, Christ has already won the victory, and they will share in that victory if they remain faithful to Him.

5. Living with an Eternal Perspective: The promise of rest and reward for the faithful reminds Christians to live with an eternal perspective. The trials of this life are temporary, but the reward for faithfulness is eternal. Believers are encouraged to focus on the hope of eternal life with God, knowing that their labors in the Lord are not in vain.

The patience and endurance of the saints described in Revelation 14:12-13 is a call to persevere in faith despite the challenges and tribulations of the end times. The saints are those who keep the commandments of God and hold fast to their faith in Jesus, trusting that their perseverance will lead to ultimate victory. This endurance is not passive but requires active faith, obedience, and unwavering commitment to Christ, even in the face of opposition.

For believers today, the call to endurance is just as relevant. Christians are encouraged to remain faithful, trusting that God's promises are sure and that their perseverance will be rewarded with eternal rest and victory. Even in the midst of trials, believers can take comfort in the knowledge that they are following in the footsteps of the saints, who have gone before them, remaining steadfast in their faith and receiving the reward of eternal life with God.

The Blessed Dead

In Revelation 14:13, following the call for the patience and endurance of the saints, we hear a comforting and reassuring message proclaimed by a voice from heaven: "Blessed are the dead who die in the Lord from now on." This statement offers a profound word of hope and encouragement for those who face martyrdom or death during the tumultuous events of the last days. It serves as a promise of rest, reward, and eternal peace for the faithful who remain steadfast in their devotion to Christ, even in the face of death.

This message is significant for the persecuted believers of John's time, as well as for all Christians who face suffering or persecution for their faith. It affirms that death is not the end, but a transition into the eternal presence of God, where rest and reward await. Those who die "in the Lord" are blessed, for their deeds will follow them, and they will find rest from their earthly labors. This passage reflects a central theme in the Christian faith: death for believers is not defeat but victory, as they pass from the struggles of this world into the eternal peace and joy of God's kingdom.

Blessed Are the Dead Who Die in the Lord

The phrase "Blessed are the dead who die in the Lord" carries deep spiritual meaning. The word "blessed" here refers to more than just happiness or good fortune; it implies divine favor and eternal joy. To be blessed in this sense means to be in a state of grace and peace, having entered into the fullness of God's promise of eternal life. For those who remain faithful to Christ, death is not something to be feared but is a doorway into the eternal blessings of God.

The qualifier "in the Lord" is crucial. This blessing is reserved for those who are united with Christ, who have placed their faith in Him and lived according to His will. To "die in the Lord" means that their life, and their death, is marked by their relationship with Christ. These are people who have persevered in their faith, who have not compromised with the corrupt systems of the world, and who have kept God's commandments despite persecution or hardship. Their faith in Christ defines their death as much as it defines their life.

This message is particularly poignant for those who face martyrdom—believers who are persecuted and killed for their faith in Jesus. In the context of Revelation, where many are pressured to worship the beast or face death, this proclamation provides a source of profound comfort. Those who die for their faith are not forgotten by God, and their sacrifice is recognized as an act of ultimate loyalty to Christ. Far from being a tragic end, their death is seen as a passage into eternal blessing.

Rest from Their Labors

The voice from heaven continues: "Yes, says the Spirit, they will rest from their labors." This promise of rest is one of the most comforting aspects of this passage. For those who have struggled, endured persecution, and labored faithfully for Christ, the promise of rest is a welcome relief. It is not simply rest from physical exhaustion but a deep, spiritual rest—a rest that signifies the end of suffering, pain, and hardship.

In the Bible, rest is often associated with God's peace and presence. From the beginning, when God rested on the seventh day after creation (Genesis 2:2-3), rest has symbolized a state of completion and satisfaction. For the saints who die in the Lord, this rest represents the completion of their earthly journey and the beginning of their eternal life in the presence of God. It is the Sabbath rest that the book of Hebrews speaks of, where believers enter into God's ultimate rest, free from the struggles and burdens of this world (Hebrews 4:9-10).

The promise of rest is especially significant for those who have endured suffering and persecution. Many of the faithful, particularly in the time of the early church, faced intense trials for their faith. They were ostracized, oppressed, and even killed for refusing to worship false gods or participate in the corrupt practices of the Roman Empire. For these believers, the idea of eternal rest would have been a powerful source of comfort, knowing that their suffering would one day come to an end and they would enter into the peace of God's kingdom.

Their Deeds Will Follow Them

The final part of this verse reads: "For their deeds will follow them." This statement emphasizes that the faithful works and sacrifices of those who die in the Lord will not be forgotten. Their deeds are not left behind but follow them into eternity, where they will be remembered and rewarded.

This speaks to the eternal significance of faithful living. The deeds of the saints—acts of love, service, sacrifice, and faithfulness—are not lost in death. Instead, they carry eternal value and will be recognized by God. The idea that "their deeds will follow them" reflects the biblical principle that what we do in this life matters in eternity. As Paul writes in 1 Corinthians 15:58, "Always give yourselves fully to the work of the Lord, because you know that your labor in the Lord is not in vain."

This also suggests that the rewards awaiting the saints in heaven are directly connected to their faithfulness on earth. While salvation is a gift of God's grace and cannot be earned by works, the Bible frequently teaches that God rewards faithful service (Matthew 25:21). The deeds of those who endure persecution and remain faithful to Christ will be honored by God in eternity. These rewards are not material but reflect the joy of being in God's presence, where their lives of faith will be celebrated and their sufferings vindicated.

Martyrdom and Eternal Hope

In the context of Revelation, this blessing upon the dead takes on additional significance because of the theme of martyrdom that runs throughout the book. Many of the early

Christians to whom John wrote faced the threat of death for their faith. They were persecuted by both the Roman authorities and by religious leaders who opposed their message. For these believers, martyrdom was not an abstract possibility but a daily reality.

The assurance that those who die in the Lord are blessed and will find rest from their labors would have been a profound encouragement. This message is particularly relevant in the context of Revelation, where the conflict between the forces of good and evil is heightened, and the persecution of believers is a prominent theme. The promise of rest and eternal reward encourages Christians to remain faithful, even unto death, knowing that their suffering will not be in vain.

This verse also reflects the hope of resurrection that is central to the Christian faith. Those who die in the Lord are not simply dead; they are blessed and will one day be resurrected to eternal life in the new heavens and new earth. Death, for believers, is not a permanent separation but a transition into eternal life with God. This truth gives Christians the strength to face persecution and death with confidence, knowing that their hope lies in the promise of resurrection and eternal life.

Spiritual Application

The message of Revelation 14:13 has profound spiritual implications for believers today:

1. Death in the Lord Is a Blessing: This passage reminds Christians that death for believers is not a defeat but a victory. Those who die in the Lord are blessed, entering into the eternal peace and rest of God's kingdom. This truth offers comfort to those who are facing death or mourning the loss of loved ones who have died in the faith.

2. The Hope of Rest: The promise of rest from their labors is a powerful encouragement for all believers who are enduring suffering or hardship for the sake of the gospel. This rest signifies more than just physical relief; it is the promise of eternal peace and joy in the presence of God. For those who are weary from the challenges of life, this promise of rest offers profound hope.

3. Eternal Significance of Our Deeds: The assurance that "their deeds will follow them" reminds Christians that their faithful works have eternal value. Acts of love, service, and sacrifice are not forgotten but will be remembered and rewarded by God. This motivates believers to live lives of faithful obedience, knowing that their efforts for the kingdom of God will have lasting significance.

4. Encouragement in the Face of Martyrdom: For Christians who face persecution, this passage offers a message

of profound encouragement. Those who suffer and die for their faith are not abandoned by God; they are blessed and will find rest in His presence. The promise of eternal reward gives believers the strength to endure persecution, knowing that their ultimate victory is assured in Christ.

5. Living with an Eternal Perspective: This passage invites Christians to live with an eternal perspective, recognizing that death is not the end but the beginning of eternal life with God. It encourages believers to focus on what truly matters: their relationship with Christ and their faithful service to His kingdom. Living with this perspective enables Christians to endure trials and challenges with hope, knowing that their future is secure in God's hands.

The proclamation of Revelation 14:13 offers a message of hope, comfort, and assurance to the blessed dead—those who die in the Lord. Far from being a tragedy, death for believers is a passage into the eternal rest and peace of God's kingdom. Their deeds will follow them, and their faithfulness will be rewarded in eternity. For those who face persecution, suffering, or death for the sake of Christ, this passage is a profound reminder that their ultimate victory is assured, and they will find eternal rest in the presence of God.

The promise of blessing, rest, and reward for those who die in the Lord encourages Christians to live with endurance and faithfulness, knowing that their labor for God is not in vain and that they will one day share in the eternal joy of His kingdom.

Spiritual Application

The message of Revelation 14:12-13 provides Christians with profound spiritual encouragement. In the face of trials, persecution, or even martyrdom, believers are reminded that their faithfulness will be rewarded and that eternal rest awaits those who remain steadfast in their devotion to God. The promise that their works will not be forgotten offers a powerful motivation to continue living in obedience to God, no matter the challenges they face. This spiritual application offers several key insights for Christians as they navigate life in a world often hostile to faith.

1. Encouragement to Endure

One of the central themes of this passage is the call for believers to endure. Endurance, in this context, means remaining firm in one's faith, even when the pressures of the world—whether through persecution, suffering, or temptation—seem overwhelming. The Christian journey is often marked by trials, and the saints are encouraged to hold fast to their faith in Jesus and keep the commandments of God despite these hardships.

The endurance of the saints is not merely about surviving difficult times but involves an active, persistent commitment to Christ. It is a daily decision to choose faithfulness over compromise, to walk in the truth of God's Word rather than conforming to the ways of the world. For Christians today, this call to endurance is just as relevant. We live in a world where cultural pressures, temptations, and distractions can easily pull us away from our devotion to God. The message of Revelation reminds us that perseverance in faith is essential for the Christian life, and it offers the hope that this endurance will lead to eternal victory.

Christians can take comfort in knowing that their endurance has eternal significance. God sees their faithfulness and honors their commitment to Him, even when it is costly. This should motivate believers to keep pressing forward, trusting that their endurance is not in vain.

2. The Promise of Eternal Rest

One of the most comforting aspects of this passage is the promise of eternal rest for those who remain faithful. The voice from heaven declares, "Blessed are the dead who die in the Lord from now on... they will rest from their labors" (Revelation 14:13). For believers, this rest is not merely physical relief from the weariness of life but a deep, spiritual rest in the presence of God. It is the fulfillment of God's promise of eternal peace and joy in His kingdom.

This promise of rest should encourage Christians to persevere through suffering. No matter how intense the trials they face in this life, they can trust that God's rest awaits them in eternity. This rest is the ultimate reward for their faithfulness, and it provides a profound hope that sustains them through their present difficulties.

For those who feel overwhelmed by the struggles of life, whether physical, emotional, or spiritual, the assurance of eternal rest is a reminder that God's peace is coming. It serves as a source of hope and encouragement, motivating believers to continue living faithfully, knowing that they will soon enter into the rest of God's kingdom.

3. Assurance That Their Works Will Not Be Forgotten

The promise that the works of the faithful will "follow them" (Revelation 14:13) is a powerful affirmation of the eternal value of our deeds. While salvation is a gift of God's grace, the Bible consistently teaches that God values and rewards the faithful works of His people. Every act of obedience, every sacrifice made for the sake of Christ, every deed done in love and service to others will be remembered and honored by God.

This assurance should inspire Christians to live lives of faithful service, knowing that their efforts are not in vain. Whether their works are seen and recognized by others or carried out in quiet, unnoticed ways, they have eternal significance in God's eyes. This truth offers great encouragement, especially to those who may feel discouraged or unnoticed in their labors for the Lord. God sees their faithfulness, and their deeds will not be forgotten.

Moreover, the fact that their works "follow them" into eternity reminds believers that their faithfulness in this life has eternal consequences. What they do for God now will matter for eternity. This should motivate Christians to invest their lives in things that have lasting value—serving others, advancing God's kingdom, and living in obedience to His will.

4. The Cost of Faithfulness

The context of this passage highlights the reality that faithfulness often comes with a cost. Many of the saints described in Revelation face persecution, suffering, and even death for their refusal to compromise their faith. The declaration that "blessed are the dead who die in the Lord" is a direct encouragement to those who face martyrdom or intense suffering for their faith. For them, death is not a defeat but the beginning of eternal victory.

While most Christians today may not face physical martyrdom, many still experience trials and hardships for their faith. Whether through social rejection, family opposition, or personal sacrifice, following Christ often involves bearing a cost. Yet the assurance of eternal rest and the promise of reward for their deeds should encourage believers to remain steadfast, even when the path is difficult.

Christians are called to remain faithful to God, even when it seems costly, knowing that God's reward far outweighs any temporary suffering they may endure. This eternal perspective helps believers to stay focused on what truly matters and to persevere in their faith, trusting that God's promises will be fulfilled.

5. Living with an Eternal Perspective

The spiritual application of this passage encourages Christians to live with an eternal perspective. In the midst of the trials and challenges of life, it is easy to become focused on the temporary, day-to-day struggles. However, the promise of eternal rest and reward invites believers to look beyond the present and to focus on the eternal kingdom of God.

Living with an eternal perspective helps Christians to prioritize what truly matters. It challenges them to invest their time, energy, and resources in things that have eternal value—serving God, loving others, and advancing His kingdom. It also helps them to endure suffering with hope, knowing that their ultimate reward lies in eternity with God.

This eternal perspective shifts the way believers approach both their joys and their trials. Rather than seeking immediate gratification or relief, they live with the understanding that eternal joy and peace await them in God's presence. This allows them to persevere with hope, knowing that their future is secure in Christ.

The spiritual application of Revelation 14:12-13 offers believers powerful encouragement to remain steadfast in their faith, no matter the cost. The promise of eternal rest and the assurance that their works will not be forgotten should motivate Christians to endure through trials, trusting that their faithfulness will be richly rewarded. This passage challenges believers to live with an eternal perspective, focusing on the things that have lasting value and remembering that their perseverance in faith has eternal significance.

For those who feel weary or discouraged, the promise of eternal rest offers profound hope. It reminds believers that their suffering is temporary and that God's peace and joy await them in eternity. As Christians continue to walk faithfully, they can take comfort in knowing that God sees their efforts, and their deeds will follow them into eternity, where they will be remembered and rewarded by their Creator.

The call to endurance and faithfulness is not merely a call to survive but to actively persevere in the work of God, trusting that their faith will lead to eternal victory in Christ.

CHAPTER 04

THE HARVEST OF THE EARTH

The final section of Revelation 14, in verses 14-20, presents a powerful and vivid depiction of the final judgment of humanity through the imagery of two harvests. These harvests symbolize the separation of the righteous from the wicked, a theme that runs throughout Scripture when discussing the ultimate destiny of humanity. The first harvest represents the gathering of the faithful and righteous, while the second symbolizes the judgment of the wicked. Together, these two harvests reflect the dual nature of God's judgment: one of redemption and reward for the faithful, and the other of wrath and punishment for those who have rejected God.

The imagery of harvest is often used in the Bible to describe judgment and salvation. In this passage, the harvest is not only the culmination of God's plan for humanity but also the moment when the justice of God is fully revealed. It serves as a final call to readiness, urging believers to live faithfully in anticipation of Christ's return, while warning those who remain in rebellion that judgment is certain.

The Son of Man and the Harvest of the Righteous

In Revelation 14:14-16, the first of the two harvests is described. The Apostle John writes, "I looked, and there before me was a white cloud, and seated on the cloud was one like a son of man with a crown of gold on his head and a sharp sickle in his hand." This image of the Son of Man seated on a cloud recalls the prophetic vision of Daniel 7:13, where the Son of Man comes with the clouds of heaven to establish God's kingdom. In this context, the Son of Man is understood to be Jesus Christ, who comes to gather the faithful into His kingdom.

The white cloud upon which the Son of Man sits is a symbol of purity and divine authority, while the golden crown on His head signifies His sovereignty and kingship. This imagery highlights Christ's role as the Lord of the harvest— the One who has the authority to execute judgment and to gather His people.

The sharp sickle in His hand is an instrument of harvest, symbolizing the act of gathering. In the ancient world, a sickle was used to reap grain at the time of harvest, and here it represents the final gathering of the righteous at the end of the age. The imagery of Christ wielding the sickle is a powerful reminder that the time of judgment has arrived, and the harvest is ripe.

In verse 15, an angel comes from the temple, calling out to the Son of Man: "Take your sickle and reap, because the time to reap has come, for the harvest of the earth is ripe." This declaration signifies that the moment of judgment has arrived. The phrase "the harvest is ripe" indicates that the time for separating the righteous from the wicked has come to its fulfillment—there is no more delay.

The harvest of the righteous in this passage is an image of salvation and redemption. The faithful, who have remained loyal to God and kept His commandments, are gathered into His eternal kingdom. This harvest represents the culmination of God's promises to His people. Just as a farmer gathers the ripened grain into the barn, so too does Christ gather the faithful into the safety of His kingdom. This is a moment of triumph and joy for believers, as they are finally brought into the eternal presence of God.

The Harvest of the Wicked: The Grapes of Wrath

In contrast to the first harvest, the second harvest described in Revelation 14:17-20 presents a terrifying picture of judgment. This second harvest is often referred to as the "harvest of the wicked" or the "grapes of wrath." While the first harvest was one of salvation for the righteous, the second harvest is one of wrath and destruction for the wicked.

In verse 17, another angel emerges from the temple, this time carrying a sharp sickle. Following this, in verse 18, a second angel comes from the altar and calls out in a loud voice to the angel with the sickle, saying, "Take your sharp sickle and gather the clusters of grapes from the earth's vine, because its grapes are ripe." This second angel coming from the altar symbolizes the authority of God's judgment. The mention of the altar may be connected to the prayers of the saints (Revelation 6:9-10) crying out for justice, and now that justice is being enacted.

The clusters of grapes and the vine of the earth represent the wicked—those who have aligned themselves with the beast and rejected God's rule. These grapes are fully ripe, meaning that the wicked have reached the fullness of their sin, and the time for judgment has arrived. The act of gathering the grapes is symbolic of the gathering of the wicked for judgment.

The scene intensifies in verses 19-20, where the angel swings his sickle and gathers the grapes, which are thrown into the great winepress of God's wrath. The winepress is a powerful metaphor for God's judgment. In the ancient world, a winepress was used to crush grapes and extract their juice.

Here, the image of a winepress filled with grapes being crushed underfoot serves as a graphic depiction of divine judgment upon the wicked.

The imagery of God's wrath is further heightened in verse 20, where it says that "they were trampled in the winepress outside the city, and blood flowed out of the press, rising as high as the horses' bridles for a distance of 1,600 stadia." The flow of blood as high as the horses' bridles and for such a great distance (approximately 180 miles) symbolizes the vastness and severity of God's judgment. The image of blood flowing from the winepress represents the complete destruction of the wicked, illustrating the inescapable consequences of rejecting God.

This final judgment of the wicked is a stark reminder of the seriousness of sin and the certainty of God's justice. The wicked, who have refused to repent and have chosen to rebel against God, will face the full measure of His wrath. This judgment is not arbitrary; it is the just response to a world that has rejected God's grace and chosen evil.

The Dual Nature of the Final Harvest

The two harvests in Revelation 14:14-20—the harvest of the righteous and the harvest of the wicked—represent the dual nature of God's final judgment. This duality emphasizes that the end of the age brings both salvation for those who have placed their faith in Christ and destruction for those who have rejected Him.

For the righteous, the harvest is a time of joy and reward. They are gathered into God's eternal kingdom, where they will experience the fullness of His presence and the peace of eternal life. This harvest is the fulfillment of God's promises to His people, who have persevered in faith and obedience.

For the wicked, however, the harvest is a time of wrath and judgment. Their rejection of God and their alignment with the forces of evil have led to their destruction. The imagery of the winepress of God's wrath serves as a powerful reminder that while God is patient and merciful, His justice will ultimately prevail. Sin will be judged, and those who have chosen to live in rebellion against God will face the consequences.

Spiritual Application

The harvest of the earth in Revelation 14 has significant spiritual implications for believers today:

1. The Importance of Readiness: The imagery of the harvest reminds Christians to be spiritually ready for the return of Christ. Just as a harvest comes when the grain or fruit is ripe, so too will Christ's return come at the appointed time. Believers are called to live in constant readiness, knowing that the final judgment could come at any moment.

This means living faithfully, keeping God's commandments, and remaining steadfast in the faith.

2. God's Justice and Mercy: The two harvests highlight the dual nature of God's character—He is both just and merciful. For the righteous, the harvest is a time of reward and salvation, but for the wicked, it is a time of wrath. This should inspire believers to remain faithful and to seek God's mercy, while also serving as a warning to those who reject Him. God's justice is certain, but so is His mercy for those who turn to Him in repentance.

3. The Urgency of Evangelism: The harvest imagery also underscores the urgency of sharing the gospel. As believers, we are called to participate in God's work of gathering the righteous by proclaiming the good news of salvation in Christ. The reality of the final judgment should compel Christians to share the gospel with those who have not yet heard or responded to it. Time is limited, and the harvest is ripe.

4. The Assurance of Victory for Believers: For those who remain faithful, the harvest is a time of victory and celebration. The gathering of the righteous into God's kingdom is the fulfillment of the hope that Christians hold onto. Despite the trials and tribulations that may come,

believers can take comfort in knowing that their ultimate destiny is to be with Christ forever.

The harvest of the earth in Revelation 14:14-20 presents a powerful image of the final judgment. The two harvests—the gathering of the righteous and the judgment of the wicked—illustrate the certainty of God's justice and the dual nature of the end times. For believers, this passage offers hope and assurance that their faithfulness will be rewarded, and they will be gathered into God's eternal kingdom. For those who have rejected God, it serves as a sobering reminder that His judgment is coming, and they must repent before it is too late.

The call to live in readiness, to share the gospel with urgency, and to trust in God's justice should motivate Christians to live faithfully in light of the coming harvest. The victory of the righteous and the judgment of the wicked are both certain, and the final harvest will reveal the fulfillment of God's plan for humanity.

The Harvest of the Righteous

In Revelation 14:14-16, the Apostle John presents a vision of the "Son of Man" seated on a white cloud with a sharp sickle in His hand, prepared to reap the harvest of the earth. This scene represents the gathering of the righteous—

those who have remained faithful to God—into His kingdom. The harvest of the righteous is a profound image of salvation and deliverance, symbolizing the moment when Christ comes to gather His people at the end of the age.

This vision, filled with rich symbolism, encapsulates the hope of believers who have persevered through trials and remained loyal to Christ. It depicts the fulfillment of God's promise to bring His people into eternal safety and joy. As the Lord of the harvest, Christ exercises His authority to separate the faithful from the world and usher them into the fullness of God's kingdom. This is a moment of victory and triumph for the righteous, as they are gathered into the eternal presence of God.

The Son of Man: Christ the Lord of the Harvest

The figure seated on the white cloud is described as "one like the Son of Man" (Revelation 14:14), a title that has deep roots in both the Old and New Testaments. This title draws from Daniel 7:13, where the Son of Man comes on the clouds of heaven, given dominion and glory by the Ancient of Days. In the New Testament, Jesus frequently referred to Himself as the Son of Man, emphasizing both His role as the Messiah and His unique identity as the Savior and Judge of the world.

The white cloud upon which the Son of Man sits symbolizes His divine purity and sovereignty, while the golden crown on His head signifies His authority and kingship. The image of Christ on the cloud reflects His role as both the Redeemer and the Judge. He is not only the One who has saved humanity through His sacrificial death and resurrection but also the One who will bring about the final judgment, separating the righteous from the wicked.

In His hand, the Son of Man holds a sharp sickle—an agricultural tool used to gather ripe crops during the harvest. The sickle symbolizes the act of gathering the righteous at the appointed time. It conveys the power and decisiveness of Christ's judgment, indicating that the time for harvesting has arrived and that the righteous will now be gathered into God's kingdom.

The Time of Harvest

In verse 15, an angel emerges from the temple and calls out to the Son of Man, saying, "Take your sickle and reap, because the time to reap has come, for the harvest of the earth is ripe." The appearance of the angel from the temple suggests that this act of harvest is carried out according to the divine will of God. The heavenly temple symbolizes God's dwelling place, from which His commands are issued. The angel, therefore, is delivering the message that the time for judgment has come and that the righteous are ready to be gathered.

The phrase "the harvest of the earth is ripe" indicates that the time is fully prepared and that the righteous have reached spiritual maturity. Throughout Scripture, the harvest is often used as a metaphor for the final gathering of people, whether for salvation or judgment (Matthew 13:24-30, Mark 4:26-29). Here, the ripeness of the harvest reflects the completion of God's redemptive work in the lives of believers. The faithful have endured, and now the time has come for them to be brought into the eternal kingdom.

The angel's message underscores the imminence of the final gathering. There is no more delay; the moment of salvation for the righteous has arrived. This scene portrays the fulfillment of God's promise to redeem His people and gather them safely into His kingdom, a promise that has been anticipated throughout the entire biblical narrative.

Christ Gathers His People

In verse 16, we read that the Son of Man swings His sickle over the earth, and the earth was harvested. This simple yet powerful action represents the final gathering of the faithful into God's kingdom. The act of harvesting the righteous is a vivid metaphor for salvation and deliverance. Christ, as the Lord of the harvest, brings His people out of the fallen world and into the eternal safety and joy of His presence.

The harvest of the righteous is not just about gathering individuals but about bringing the entire people of God—those who have remained loyal to Christ, who have kept His commandments, and who have not compromised with the corrupt systems of the world—into the fullness of their salvation. This moment of harvest is the culmination of their faith, hope, and endurance.

This image of Christ gathering His people is a fulfillment of prophecy. In Matthew 24:30-31, Jesus speaks of His return, saying, "They will see the Son of Man coming on the clouds of heaven with power and great glory. And He will send His angels with a loud trumpet call, and they will gather His elect from the four winds, from one end of the heavens to the other." This gathering of the elect is the final act of God's redemptive plan for humanity, bringing the faithful into the eternal life that Christ has promised.

Salvation and Deliverance

The harvest of the righteous is a moment of salvation and deliverance for believers. It is the moment when Christ comes to deliver His people from the fallen world, to free them from the effects of sin, suffering, and death, and to bring them into the eternal joy of God's kingdom. For those who have endured the trials and tribulations described in Revelation, this is the moment of vindication. The faithful are now rescued from the powers of evil and are brought into the eternal peace of God's presence.

For the righteous, the harvest is the fulfillment of hope. Throughout their lives, they have looked forward to this moment, trusting in God's promises and enduring hardships for the sake of Christ. Now, they are gathered into His kingdom, where they will experience eternal life in the presence of God. The harvest is the culmination of the redemptive work of Christ, who through His death and resurrection made it possible for believers to be reconciled to God and brought into His eternal kingdom.

This scene also provides assurance that Christ's promises of deliverance are true. Despite the hardships, persecution, and challenges that believers face, the harvest demonstrates that their faithfulness will be rewarded. It is a moment of triumph for the saints, who are now fully redeemed and delivered from the power of sin and death.

Spiritual Application

The harvest of the righteous in Revelation 14:14-16 carries deep spiritual significance for believers:

1. Christ as the Lord of the Harvest: The image of the Son of Man wielding the sickle reminds Christians that Christ is in control of the final judgment. He is the One who will gather His people at the appointed time. This truth should

give believers confidence that their salvation is secure in Him and that He will faithfully fulfill His promises to gather His people into His eternal kingdom.

2. The Importance of Endurance: The harvest of the righteous emphasizes the need for perseverance in the Christian life. The faithful who are gathered in this scene are those who have remained loyal to Christ despite the trials and tribulations of the world. Believers today are encouraged to endure in faith, knowing that Christ will ultimately gather them into His kingdom if they remain steadfast.

3. The Hope of Salvation: This passage offers profound hope to Christians who are suffering or facing persecution. The promise of the final harvest assures believers that their suffering is not in vain and that they will one day be gathered into the eternal presence of God. The harvest is a symbol of the ultimate victory and deliverance that awaits those who remain faithful to Christ.

4. Living in Readiness: The imagery of the harvest serves as a reminder to live in constant readiness for Christ's return. Just as a farmer waits for the harvest, believers must live with the anticipation that Christ could return at any moment. This calls for lives of faithfulness, obedience, and devotion, as believers await the day when Christ will gather His people into His kingdom.

5. Assurance of Redemption: For those who have placed their faith in Christ, the harvest of the righteous is a powerful reminder that they are secure in God's hands. No matter what trials or difficulties they face, they can be confident that Christ will deliver them in the end. The harvest is a symbol of the complete and final redemption that believers have in Christ.

The harvest of the righteous in Revelation 14:14-16 is a powerful image of salvation and deliverance. It portrays the moment when Christ, the Son of Man, gathers His faithful people into His kingdom at the end of the age. For the righteous, this harvest represents the fulfillment of God's promises, the reward for their endurance, and their final deliverance from the trials and tribulations of the world.

As Christians reflect on this passage, they are reminded to live in faithfulness and readiness, trusting that Christ will one day gather them into His eternal kingdom. The hope of the final harvest encourages believers to persevere through trials, knowing that their faithfulness will be rewarded, and they will share in the eternal joy and peace of God's kingdom.

The Harvest of the Wicked

In Revelation 14:17-20, the second harvest described by the Apostle John presents a powerful and terrifying image of God's final judgment on the wicked. This second harvest contrasts sharply with the harvest of the righteous in the previous verses. While the righteous are gathered into Christ's kingdom, the wicked are harvested for judgment and are cast into the winepress of God's wrath. The vivid imagery of this passage conveys the severity and inevitability of divine judgment on those who have rejected God and lived in rebellion.

The grapes of the earth symbolize the wicked, who have reached the fullness of their sin, and the winepress represents the destructive judgment that awaits them. The image of blood flowing from the winepress, rising as high as a horse's bridle, emphasizes the total devastation and finality of God's judgment. This passage serves as a sobering reminder of the consequences of sin and the certainty of divine justice.

The Angel with the Sharp Sickle

In Revelation 14:17, John sees another angel emerge, this time from the temple in heaven, carrying a sharp sickle. The fact that this angel comes from the temple indicates that this judgment is being carried out according to God's divine authority and is part of His righteous plan. The sickle symbolizes the tool of harvest, but in this case, it is not a harvest of salvation but a harvest of judgment.

Unlike the Son of Man in the first harvest, who represents Christ gathering the faithful, this angel is sent to carry out the grim task of gathering the wicked. The appearance of this angel with a sickle signifies that the time for judgment has come and that the wicked are ready to be gathered for their destruction.

The Grapes of the Earth: The Wicked Ready for Judgment

In verse 18, another angel emerges from the altar, calling out in a loud voice to the angel with the sickle: "Take your sharp sickle and gather the clusters of grapes from the earth's vine, because its grapes are ripe." The angel from the altar symbolizes the authority of God's judgment and is possibly connected to the prayers of the saints, who in earlier visions cry out to God for justice (Revelation 6:9-10).

The clusters of grapes represent the wicked—those who have rejected God's offer of salvation, who have aligned themselves with the beast and the corrupt systems of the world. These grapes are described as "ripe," which symbolizes that the time for their judgment has come. Just as ripened grapes are gathered to be crushed in a winepress, the wicked are now fully prepared to face the consequences of their rebellion. The vine of the earth refers to the world's sinful systems and influences that have led people away from God and toward destruction.

This gathering of the wicked is not a random or arbitrary event—it is the result of their rejection of God and their alignment with the forces of evil. The imagery of ripeness indicates that their sin has reached its fullness, and now the time for patience and mercy has ended. The harvest of the wicked is God's response to the injustice, immorality, and idolatry that have defined their lives.

The Great Winepress of God's Wrath

In verse 19, the angel swings his sickle and gathers the grapes, throwing them into the great winepress of God's wrath. The image of a winepress is a powerful symbol of judgment in the Bible. In ancient times, a winepress was used to crush grapes and extract their juice, but here, the crushing of the grapes represents the destruction of the wicked under the weight of God's wrath.

The winepress of God's wrath refers to the intensity and finality of God's judgment. The wicked, symbolized by the clusters of grapes, are thrown into this great winepress to be trampled underfoot, emphasizing the inescapability of divine justice. The use of a winepress to depict judgment is a metaphor for the complete and total destruction that awaits the wicked. It is a vivid and violent image, conveying that

God's wrath is not something that can be avoided or minimized—it is total and irreversible.

This imagery also echoes prophetic warnings from the Old Testament, such as in Isaiah 63:3, where God is described as trampling His enemies in a winepress, and their lifeblood is poured out. The idea of God's wrath being poured out like wine is a consistent biblical theme, representing His righteous judgment on sin and rebellion (Jeremiah 25:15-16).

The Blood from the Winepress

The most striking and terrifying image comes in verse 20, where John describes the aftermath of this judgment: "They were trampled in the winepress outside the city, and blood flowed out of the press, rising as high as the horses' bridles for a distance of 1,600 stadia." This graphic image symbolizes the severity and magnitude of God's judgment.

- Blood flowing from the winepress: The image of blood flowing from the winepress suggests the total destruction of the wicked. The blood represents the consequence of sin and the finality of God's wrath. The flow of blood as high as a horse's bridle (approximately four to five feet high) emphasizes the sheer volume of this judgment. It is not a small or isolated event but a massive outpouring of divine justice.

- 1,600 stadia: The distance of 1,600 stadia (approximately 180 miles) suggests the vast scope of this judgment. Some scholars suggest that this number symbolizes completeness or universality, indicating that no part of the earth or its wicked inhabitants will escape the judgment. The image of blood flowing for such a great distance emphasizes the global and far-reaching nature of God's wrath on the wicked.

The fact that this judgment takes place "outside the city" may also be significant. In the Old Testament, sacrifices for sin were often made outside the camp or city (Leviticus 16:27), and Jesus was crucified outside the city of Jerusalem (Hebrews 13:12). This detail might point to the fact that the wicked are judged outside of God's holy city, symbolizing their exclusion from His kingdom and His presence. The city may represent the place of safety and salvation for the righteous, while the outside represents the realm of judgment and destruction.

The Finality of God's Wrath

The imagery in Revelation 14:17-20 leaves no doubt about the finality of God's judgment on the wicked. The grapes of wrath are fully ripe, and their time of judgment has come. The winepress of God's wrath conveys the inescapable consequences of sin and rebellion against God. The blood that flows from the winepress represents the total destruction of those who have aligned themselves with the forces of evil, emphasizing that God's judgment is both just and severe.

This passage serves as a warning to all who persist in rebellion against God. It underscores the reality that God's patience will not last forever, and there will come a time when His judgment will be fully unleashed. The severity of the imagery reminds readers of the seriousness of sin and the certainty of divine justice.

Spiritual Application

The harvest of the wicked in Revelation 14:17-20 has important spiritual applications for Christians today:

1. The Reality of God's Judgment: This passage underscores the reality that God's judgment is certain. The imagery of the winepress of wrath reminds us that while God is patient, His judgment on sin is inevitable. This should lead believers to take sin seriously and to live lives that are pleasing to God, knowing that rebellion against Him leads to destruction.

2. The Urgency of Repentance: The vision of the grapes of wrath emphasizes that the time for repentance is limited. The ripening of the grapes represents the fullness of sin, and once that time has come, judgment will follow. This should inspire a sense of urgency in repenting of sin and

turning to God, as well as in sharing the gospel with others before it is too late.

3. God's Justice and Righteousness: The winepress of God's wrath reflects the justice and righteousness of God's character. While the image is terrifying, it is also a reminder that God's judgment is justified—the wicked face the consequences of their choices, and God's justice prevails. For believers, this is a source of hope, knowing that evil will not go unpunished, and God will ultimately bring justice to the world.

4. The Consequences of Rebellion: The graphic image of blood flowing from the winepress highlights the seriousness of rebellion against God. It serves as a reminder that there are eternal consequences for rejecting God's offer of salvation and choosing to live in sin. This should motivate believers to remain faithful to God and to share the message of salvation with those who are lost.

The harvest of the wicked in Revelation 14:17-20 presents a sobering and terrifying picture of God's final judgment. The image of the winepress of God's wrath, filled with the ripened grapes of the earth, symbolizes the destruction of the wicked who have rejected God's authority and chosen to align themselves with the forces of evil. The graphic imagery of blood flowing from the winepress emphasizes the severity and finality of this judgment.

For believers, this passage serves as a warning of the reality of God's judgment and the consequences of sin. It also provides a reminder of the urgency of repentance and the need to share the message of salvation with a world that is ripe for judgment. While the harvest of the righteous brings salvation and deliverance, the harvest of the wicked brings destruction and wrath, demonstrating the justice and righteousness of God's judgment.

Spiritual Application

The dual harvest depicted in Revelation 14 offers a profound spiritual lesson for Christians today, reminding believers of the ultimate separation between the righteous and the wicked at the time of God's final judgment. This imagery conveys the sobering reality that a day will come when the harvest of the earth will take place, and every person will face either salvation or judgment. The harvest of the righteous represents the joyful gathering of those who have remained faithful to Christ, while the harvest of the wicked reflects the inevitable judgment on those who have rejected God's authority and persisted in rebellion.

This stark portrayal of God's justice and mercy calls believers to deep self-reflection, encouraging them to consider their standing before God and their relationship with

Christ. It serves as a reminder that the decisions we make in this life have eternal consequences, and it challenges Christians to live faithfully, knowing that the day of harvest is coming.

1. The Reality of Final Judgment

The dual harvest is a powerful reminder that the world is moving toward a definitive moment of judgment, when God will separate the righteous from the wicked. This is a consistent theme throughout the Bible, with Jesus Himself teaching about the final separation between the wheat and the tares (Matthew 13:24-30) and the sheep and the goats (Matthew 25:31-46). In the end, no one will escape this judgment, and every person will be gathered either into God's kingdom or into His wrath.

For believers, this reality should prompt a sense of urgency and sobriety. The harvest is coming, and each individual will be held accountable for the choices they have made in response to God's offer of salvation. This calls for personal reflection: Are we living in a way that reflects our allegiance to Christ? Have we fully embraced the gospel and lived in obedience to God's Word, or have we allowed the distractions and temptations of the world to pull us away from Him?

This chapter challenges Christians to evaluate their spiritual lives, recognizing that the harvest of the righteous is a promise of reward for those who persevere in faith, while the harvest of the wicked is a warning for those who continue in rebellion. It reminds us that the final judgment is certain, and we must be prepared.

2. A Call to Faithfulness

The imagery of the harvest of the righteous serves as an encouragement to remain faithful and persevere in the face of trials. The righteous are those who have continued to keep the commandments of God and the faith of Jesus (Revelation 14:12). This faithfulness is not simply about maintaining a set of beliefs, but about living a life of obedience, integrity, and devotion to Christ, even when it is costly.

For Christians, this means that faith is more than just a profession of belief—it must be evident in the way we live, the decisions we make, and the priorities we set. The day of harvest is coming, and God will gather those who have remained loyal to Him. This should inspire believers to live with endurance, knowing that their faithfulness will be rewarded, and that no sacrifice made for Christ will be in vain.

The call to faithfulness is especially important in a world where compromise, distraction, and temptation are constant. The dual harvest reminds believers that spiritual integrity and devotion to God are essential in a world that often promotes self-interest, materialism, and rebellion against God's authority. It encourages Christians to remain vigilant and stay true to their faith, even when the world pressures them to conform to its ways.

3. The Urgency of Repentance

The harvest of the wicked in Revelation 14 is a powerful reminder of the consequences of rejecting God. The imagery of the grapes being gathered and thrown into the winepress of God's wrath illustrates the terrifying reality of judgment for those who have persisted in sin and rebellion. This vivid picture should stir a sense of urgency for repentance, both in our own lives and in our witness to others.

For those who have not yet turned to God, the message is clear: the time to repent is now. The wicked are described as "ripe," meaning that the time for judgment has come, and there is no more delay. This reflects the biblical teaching that there will be a time when God's patience reaches its end and the opportunity for repentance is over. Christians are reminded that today is the day of salvation (2 Corinthians 6:2) and that we should not delay in turning to God or sharing the gospel with others.

For believers, this should also deepen our commitment to evangelism. The reality of the coming judgment should motivate us to share the message of Christ with those who are lost. We know that God desires all people to come to repentance (2 Peter 3:9), and as followers of

Christ, we are called to be ambassadors of reconciliation (2 Corinthians 5:20), proclaiming the good news that salvation is available through faith in Jesus Christ. The urgency of the dual harvest reminds us that time is limited, and we must act with compassion and conviction to reach others with the gospel.

4. Living with an Eternal Perspective

The dual harvest also calls believers to live with an eternal perspective, recognizing that the choices we make in this life have eternal significance. The separation of the righteous and the wicked in the final harvest reveals that the present world, with all its distractions, temptations, and challenges, is temporary. What truly matters is how we live in response to God's eternal kingdom.

Living with an eternal perspective means that we prioritize spiritual growth, obedience to God, and faithfulness to His mission above the fleeting pleasures or pressures of the world. It means viewing our lives not through the lens of earthly success, comfort, or status, but through the lens of God's eternal plan. We are called to invest in what lasts—our relationship with God, the love we show to others, and the work we do for His kingdom.

The reality of the coming harvest should inspire believers to focus on the things that have eternal value. This involves aligning our lives with God's purposes, making decisions that honor Him, and keeping our eyes fixed on the eternal reward that awaits those who remain faithful. As Jesus said in Matthew 6:19-20, "Do not store up for yourselves treasures on earth, where moths and vermin destroy, and where thieves break in and steal. But store up for yourselves treasures in heaven." The dual harvest reminds us to live with this heavenly perspective, seeking first the kingdom of God and His righteousness (Matthew 6:33).

5. The Justice and Mercy of God

Finally, the dual harvest in Revelation 14 highlights the justice and mercy of God. The harvest of the righteous demonstrates God's faithfulness to His promises and His desire to bring His people into the fullness of salvation. It is an expression of His mercy, as He gathers those who have trusted in Christ into His kingdom. This gives believers assurance that their faith is not in vain and that God will bring about justice and redemption for His people.

On the other hand, the harvest of the wicked reflects the justice of God. While the image of the winepress of God's wrath is sobering, it reminds us that God's judgment is righteous and that He will not leave sin unpunished. For those who have rejected God's offer of salvation, the harvest represents the consequences of their choices. God's justice is not arbitrary but is based on the decisions people make in response to Him. This truth underscores the seriousness of our spiritual choices and the reality of accountability before God.

For Christians, this balance of justice and mercy should shape our understanding of God's character and inspire both gratitude for His grace and reverence for His holiness. It reminds us that while God is merciful and patient, offering salvation to all, He is also just, and there will be a time when judgment comes.

The spiritual application of the dual harvest in Revelation 14 provides believers with a compelling call to self-reflection, faithfulness, and urgency. The passage reminds us that a day is coming when God will judge the world, separating the righteous from the wicked. For Christians, this should lead to a deeper commitment to living faithfully before God, knowing that the day of harvest is near.

Believers are encouraged to persevere in their faith, trusting that Christ will gather them into His kingdom, while the reality of judgment should stir a sense of urgency in sharing the gospel with those who are lost. The dual harvest also calls us to live with an eternal perspective, prioritizing God's kingdom and investing in what truly lasts.

Ultimately, this chapter of Revelation serves as a reminder of both God's justice and mercy. It calls us to prepare for the coming harvest by living in obedience to

Christ, with hearts full of gratitude for His grace and a commitment to faithfully serve Him until the end.

CONCLUSION

Revelation Chapter 14 presents a dramatic and vivid picture of the final stages of God's redemptive plan for humanity. Through its striking imagery, the chapter emphasizes both the hope of salvation for the faithful and the certainty of judgment for the wicked. It portrays the ultimate victory of Christ over the forces of evil, offering both encouragement and warning to Christians living in anticipation of the end times.

The chapter opens with the powerful vision of the Lamb standing on Mount Zion, accompanied by the 144,000, representing the redeemed who have remained faithful to God despite the trials and temptations of the world. This vision serves as a profound reminder of the assurance of salvation for those who follow Christ, the Lamb of God, and live-in obedience to His commandments. It is a call to endurance and faithfulness, especially for believers facing persecution and adversity.

The three angelic messages that follow in the chapter are both a proclamation and a warning. The first angel announces the everlasting gospel, calling all people to worship God as Creator and to prepare for the hour of His judgment. The second angel declares the fall of Babylon, symbolizing the inevitable collapse of the world's corrupt systems and the ultimate defeat of evil. The third angel delivers a dire warning to those who worship the beast and receive its mark, reminding readers of the eternal consequences of aligning with the forces of evil.

The chapter culminates in the dramatic imagery of the dual harvest, where the righteous are gathered into Christ's kingdom, and the wicked are cast into the winepress of God's wrath. This final separation between the faithful and the rebellious underscores the certainty of judgment and the seriousness of sin. The harvest of the earth reveals that, in the end, every individual will face either salvation or judgment based on their response to God's offer of grace.

For believers, Revelation 14 is a call to perseverance, faithfulness, and urgency. The promise of eternal life for those who follow the Lamb provides comfort and hope, while the warning of judgment for those who reject God compels Christians to proclaim the gospel with urgency in a world heading toward its final judgment. The chapter invites believers to reflect on their lives, to live in holiness and obedience, and to maintain a heavenly perspective, knowing that the current world will pass away, but God's kingdom will endure forever.

As we meditate on the truths of Revelation 14, we are reminded that the world as we know it is temporary and that God's kingdom is eternal. Christ will return, and His will shall be done on earth as it is in heaven. For those who have trusted in Christ and followed Him faithfully, there is the promise of eternal life and the joy of standing with Him in victory. For those who have rejected God's offer of salvation, the chapter offers a sobering glimpse of the wrath to come.

In light of these profound truths, let us strive to live in a way that honors God, sharing the message of the everlasting gospel with a world in need, and looking forward with hope to the return of our Savior, when He will gather His people and establish His kingdom in full.

REFERENCES

1. The Holy Bible, New King James Version. (1982). Nashville, TN: Thomas Nelson, Inc.

- The primary source of all biblical references, including the passages from Revelation 14 and other related scripture (Matthew 13:24-30, Isaiah 63:3, Daniel 7:13, etc.).

2. Beale, G. K. (1999). The Book of Revelation: A Commentary on the Greek Text (New International Greek Testament Commentary). Grand Rapids, MI: Eerdmans.

- Beale's comprehensive work provides deep exegesis on the imagery and symbolism in Revelation, particularly the meaning of the harvest imagery and the dual judgments found in Chapter 14.

3. Mounce, Robert H. (1997). The Book of Revelation (Revised Edition). Grand Rapids, MI: Eerdmans.

- Mounce's analysis offers insight into the eschatological themes of Revelation 14 and a balanced perspective on the judgment and salvation motifs.

4. Osborne, Grant R. (2002). Revelation (Baker Exegetical Commentary on the New Testament). Grand Rapids, MI: Baker Academic.

- Osborne's commentary elaborates on the meaning of the three angels' messages and the dual harvest, connecting them to the broader theology of Revelation.

5. Johnson, Dennis E. (2001). Triumph of the Lamb: A Commentary on Revelation. Phillipsburg, NJ: P&R Publishing.

- This work provides a helpful overview of the structure and theology of Revelation, with specific emphasis on the victory of Christ and its implications for the church.

6. Keener, Craig S. (2000). The NIV Application Commentary: Revelation. Grand Rapids, MI: Zondervan.

- Keener's commentary applies the themes of Revelation 14 to contemporary Christian life, highlighting the importance of faithfulness, evangelism, and endurance.

7. Patterson, Paige (2012). The New American Commentary: Revelation. Nashville, TN: B&H Publishing Group.

- Patterson offers a pastoral and theological interpretation of the judgment imagery and the call to repentance found in Revelation 14, emphasizing its practical application for believers.

8. Ladd, George Eldon (1972). A Commentary on the Revelation of John. Grand Rapids, MI: Eerdmans.

- Ladd's commentary provides a foundational understanding of the symbolism in Revelation, particularly the Son of Man imagery and the implications of the final harvest.

These references offer a mix of biblical commentary, theological insight, and practical application, helping to enrich the understanding of Revelation 14 and its powerful message.

A

- The fall of Babylon, 37

- Corruption and rebellion against God, 37-38

- Spiritual application of Babylon's fall, 41

C

- Christ:

  - The Lamb on Mount Zion, 14-18

  - Victory over evil, 16-17

  - The Son of Man: Judgment and harvest, 49-53, 58-60

  - Ultimate authority in judgment, 57-59

  - Gathering of the righteous, 50-53

- Corruption:

  - Symbolism of Babylon's corruption, 37-38

  - Worldly powers in rebellion against God, 37, 39

D

- Dual harvest:

  - Separation of righteous and wicked, 58-61

  - Harvest of the righteous: Salvation, 49-54

  - Harvest of the wicked: Judgment, 55-60

  - Spiritual application, 62-65

- The everlasting gospel proclaimed by the first angel, 35-36

- Urgency of repentance and salvation, 41-44

H

- Harvest:
  - Dual harvest imagery in Revelation 14, 49-61
  - Harvest of the righteous: Salvation and gathering into God's kingdom, 49-54
  - Harvest of the wicked: Judgment and the winepress of God's wrath, 55-60
  - Spiritual application: Call to readiness and faithfulness, 62-65

J

- Judgment:
  - The final judgment in Revelation 14, 58-61
  - Separation of the righteous and wicked, 58-60
  - Winepress of God's wrath: Symbolism of judgment, 55-60
  - Certainty of divine justice, 63-65

L

www.ingramcontent.com/pod-product-compliance
Lightning Source LLC
Chambersburg PA
CBHW061302120726
48001CB00001B/431